The Rise of Dogwhistle Politics

THE RISE

OF DOGWHISTLE

POLITICS

DEBORAH CAMERON

polity

First published by Polity Press in 2025.

Polity Press
65 Bridge Street
Cambridge CB2 1UR, UK

Polity Press
111 River Street
Hoboken, NJ 07030, USA

ISBN-13: 978-1-5095-6900-7 – hardback

A catalogue record for this book is available from the British Library.

Library of Congress Control Number: 2025940805

Typeset in 11 on 14pt Warnock Pro
by Cheshire Typesetting Ltd, Cuddington, Cheshire
Printed and bound in Great Britain by CPI Group (UK) Ltd, Croydon

The publisher has used its best endeavours to ensure that the URLs for external websites referred to in this book are correct and active at the time of going to press. However, the publisher has no responsibility for the websites and can make no guarantee that a site will remain live or that the content is or will remain appropriate.

Every effort has been made to trace all copyright holders, but if any have been overlooked the publisher will be pleased to include any necessary credits in any subsequent reprint or edition.

For further information on Polity, visit our website:
politybooks.com

Contents

1

The Rise of Dogwhistle Politics

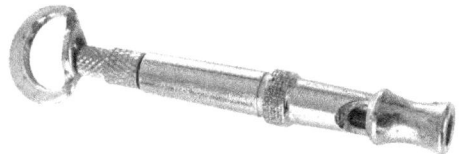

A few years ago I started to get the feeling that everyone was talking about dogwhistles. Politicians in the House of Commons attacked their opponents' dogwhistle tactics; newspaper columnists warned about the dangers of dogwhistle politics; activists and academics composed lengthy Twitter threads or blog posts explaining why something apparently innocent – an everyday word or phrase, a scarf, a cuddly toy, a social media account sharing pictures of classical buildings[1] – was really a dogwhistle for racism, antisemitism or transphobia.

It's true, of course, that once you've noticed something you will often start to see examples of it everywhere. That isn't necessarily because there's more of it around; it might be simply because you're paying it more attention. But in this case there was some reason to think the trend I'd noticed was real. There's evidence that the frequency of the term *dogwhistle* in published sources like books and newspapers has increased steadily since the turn of the millennium, and that it's risen even more sharply since the mid-2010s.[2] That's not to say it's 'everywhere', or that 'everyone' is using it: it belongs to the vocabulary of politics, so if politics is not your thing you may not come across it very often. I, on the other hand, am exactly the kind of person who's most likely to come across it. I'm interested in politics and I read a lot about it; I'm an active user of some social media platforms, and a more than occasional lurker on others, whose users spend a lot of time discussing political issues. But in addition, I'm a linguist – more specifically a sociolinguist, someone who studies the relationship between linguistic and social phenomena. Sociolinguists are interested in, among other things, the way changes in the use of language over time may be related to larger social shifts. We're probably more likely than the average person to notice this kind of change and ask what might be behind it.

That's what I want to ask about *dogwhistle*. Why is there more talk about dogwhistling now than there was ten or fifteen years ago? Who is using the term, in what contexts, to mean what, and for what purposes? What might that tell us about, and how might it affect, the political culture(s) in which it's happening? In this book I'll be pondering those questions, and trying to provide some answers.

This is, deliberately, a different angle from the one taken in most writing about dogwhistles by linguists, philosophers and other academic experts. Whereas they have typically concentrated on dogwhistling itself – what it is, how it works, what it accomplishes for those who use it – I am interested in how people talk *about* dogwhistling. As we'll see in a later chapter, the meaning of the term has broadened over time: many English speakers now use it to describe communications which are not dogwhistles by the original definition, but which are felt to have some of the same qualities – in particular, expressing prejudice or hatred. But while the broadening of a term's meaning may go along with a rise in its frequency (the more cases you can apply it to, the more opportunities there will be to use it), on its own I don't think that can explain why references to dogwhistling have increased so markedly since the mid-2010s. To me it seems likely that both changes – the broadening of *dogwhistle*'s meaning and the rise in its frequency of occurrence – reflect the same underlying trend: a recent growth in concern about prejudiced or hateful speech. If so, that's another thing that interests me. The concern itself isn't new; if we are now talking about it more, or differently, why is that? What larger social and political shifts might it be linked to, and what ideas about language lie behind it?

My interest in those questions means that this book – in spite of its title – will not be exclusively about dogwhistles. In my view there is more to 'the rise of dogwhistle politics' than just an increase in dogwhistling or in talk about dogwhistling; what I also want to draw attention to is the rise of an attitude or mindset in which the *idea* of the dogwhistle has a particular significance, exerting a powerful influence on political discourse generally. Sometimes the idea is referenced directly (e.g., when one party to an argument accuses another of dogwhistling), but it doesn't have to be made explicit. Even when the message being debated or criticized is not technically a dogwhistle, and even when no one is calling it a dogwhistle, the idea for which *dogwhistle* has become shorthand – that of a hateful and harmful message cloaked in seemingly innocuous words – may implicitly shape its interpretation. But when the qualities that define the dogwhistle (such as deceitfulness and hate) are projected onto all kinds of political communications, the result is a tendency which has been aptly described as favouring 'the worst-faith reading of everything'.[3] Rather than trying to understand what's being expressed, this way of reading looks for reasons to condemn it. In some cases that's deliberate, the product of actual bad faith, but in others it seems more like a habit or a reflex, automatic and unthinking.

In the chapters that follow I'll ask where this attitude comes from and what consequences it has – questions which will lead me, especially in the second half of the book, to move beyond the specific issue of dogwhistling and address more general questions about language, hate and harm. That, in turn, will prompt me to consider some other types of communication that raise those questions. Though they are different from dogwhistles, and go by different names (like 'slurs' or 'microaggressions'), I'll suggest that their treatment reflects the same assumptions about politics and language.

But dogwhistling itself will be my starting point. At this juncture, then, I want to take a step back and consider what (at least in theory) dogwhistles are. If you've chosen to read this book you're probably at least somewhat familiar with the concept and the term, but it's still useful to say something about where *dogwhistle* came from and what it originally meant.

Dogwhistling: a brief history

Though it's difficult to pin down the exact origins of *dogwhistle* as a political term, it's been suggested that the first people to use it in something like the sense we use it now were opinion pollsters in the 1980s, who noticed that apparently very minor differences in the wording of their questions could make a significant difference to the responses people gave. For instance, when two US polling organizations (Gallup and the National Opinion Research Center (NORC)) asked people to say how happy they were, giving them the options *very happy/ pretty happy/not too happy* (NORC) or *very happy/fairly happy/not too happy* (Gallup), it turned out to make a difference whether the middle option contained *pretty* or *fairly*. A significantly higher proportion of respondents chose 'pretty happy' in the NORC poll than chose 'fairly happy' in the Gallup poll: when 'fairly happy' was the intermediate choice people were more likely to opt for 'very happy'.[4] This was labelled a 'dogwhistle effect' – an allusion to the ultrasonic dogwhistle whose high-pitched sound is inaudible to humans – because respondents seemed to be hearing something in the words which the question-designers had not heard. For the pollsters this effect was both unintended and (since it could potentially skew their findings) unwanted. But the term *dogwhistle* would subsequently be adopted to describe cases where the effect was harnessed intentionally to send a coded political message.

Many discussions of dogwhistling in this sense have focused on its use, particularly in US politics, as a strategy for exploiting racial resentment among white voters.[5] As the veteran Republican strategist Lee Atwater explained in an interview in 1981,[6] until the late 1960s politicians could appeal to racism openly; but after the passage of the Civil Rights Act which ended racial segregation it became less socially acceptable, and therefore less politically advantageous, to use overtly racist language. The solution was to shift to what Atwater called 'abstract' terms – words and phrases which did not refer explicitly to race, but which could still be understood as coded references to it. Politicians might talk, for instance, about 'law and order', or 'states' rights' (a formula historically used in the southern states of the US to defend slavery and later segregation). Because these formulas didn't mention race directly, speakers who used them could fend off accusations of racism by insisting that their point had nothing to do with race: they were simply responding to concerns about crime, or expressing their belief that the federal government should not encroach on the prerogatives of individual states. To many listeners these denials would seem reasonable, or at least difficult to dismiss out of hand: you don't have to be a racist to think that crime is a problem, or that the federal government has too much power. But there would also be people in the audience who understood that the speaker was, in fact, talking about race, and who responded to that positively because they shared his racist views.[7] Those people were the strategy's targets: the goal was to let them know a politician was on their side, but without making it so obvious that less racist voters would be repelled. This is another instance of the 'dogwhistle effect' whereby some listeners hear things in a message that others don't. But in the political context it's a feature, not a bug.

A political dogwhistle, then, is classically defined as a message[8] with a hidden meaning or subtext that is intended to be noticed by some listeners without attracting the attention of others. Everyone will pick up the ostensible or surface meaning (e.g., 'if I'm elected I will restore law and order'), but a subset of the audience will also discern a less obvious secondary meaning, a proposition which is not stated explicitly but can be inferred from the use of certain codewords, phrases or images (e.g., 'restore law and order' as a code for 'more aggressive policing of black neighbourhoods'). Typically this secondary meaning appeals to prejudices whose open expression would attract disapproval, while giving the sender of the message 'plausible deniability' ('where did I say anything about black neighbourhoods? If you think that's what I meant then you're the one who's racist').

Though we'll see later that the meaning of *dogwhistle* has evolved, the 'classic' definition is still the one that most commonly appears in dictionaries. The UK-based *Oxford English Dictionary* (OED) defines *dogwhistle*, used in the political sense, as 'a statement or expression which in addition to its ostensible meaning has a further interpretation or connotation intended to be understood only by a specific target audience'. Merriam-Webster, a leading US dictionary, goes with 'an expression or statement that has a secondary meaning intended to be understood only by a particular group of people'. As well as being very similar, these definitions are both quite general: neither specifically mentions, for instance, that the secondary meaning is one that appeals to prejudice. However, in both dictionaries that point is clarified by the examples which are reproduced from published sources to illustrate the real-world usage of *dogwhistle*. In the OED, for instance, the first and earliest example comes from a 1995 article in a Canadian newspaper which referred to the phrase 'special interest' as 'an all-purpose dog-whistle that those fed up with feminists, minorities, the undeserving poor hear loud and clear'.

Merriam-Webster's online entry includes a section headed 'How to use *dog whistle* in a sentence' that contains a large number of examples drawn from texts published after 2016 – a moment when, as I mentioned earlier, there's evidence that the term's frequency in printed texts was rising sharply. The examples in this section suggest that the increase in its use was at least partly connected to the rise of Donald Trump. Trump is mentioned directly in eleven examples out of thirty, taken from sources that range from NBC News ('Trump's Juneteenth Tulsa rally might have been a mistake – or a racist dog whistle') to *Teen Vogue* ('the Trump hat is sometimes a dog whistle of barbaric white supremacy, and that is a massive problem'). Though Trump was not the first US president to be criticized for dogwhistling,[9] his emergence as a serious contender for the presidency brought renewed attention to the issue. In July 2016, just after the Republican convention where he was officially nominated, the *Columbia Journalism Review*'s 'Language corner' feature noted that two expressions had become ubiquitous in reporting on his campaign: one was *dumpster fire* and the other was *dogwhistle*.[10]

The examples given in dictionary entries illustrate two other points of interest. First, while at one level *dogwhistle* is a descriptive term, a name for a particular rhetorical strategy, in actual use it has a clear, and strongly negative, evaluative loading. Describing a message as a dogwhistle always implies disapproval, both of the message and by extension of its sender. Second, the term is used predominantly by 'progressive' (liberal or leftist) commentators to criticize messages that come from the political right. Among the many illustrative quotations in Merriam-Webster's entry, the only one that doesn't fit this template is a complaint about it: 'Democrats and liberals sometimes have gone to ridiculous lengths to portray speech by Republicans and conservatives as dog whistles responsible for inciting unstable people to carry out violent acts.'

Why is dogwhistling so strongly associated with the political right? It's not because indirect or coded messaging is inherently a right-wing strategy: it has been a feature of all kinds of political communication for centuries (as well as of many kinds of communication which are not directly political[11]). Rather it's because the term *dogwhistle*, and the analysis that goes with it, belong to a liberal or leftist tradition of language criticism which looks at language as a tool of oppression, used by dominant groups to maintain their power and to make it appear legitimate.

Though complaints about politicians' manipulative and self-serving rhetoric go back to antiquity (when their targets were 'demagogues' like Cleon of Athens, who was accused of using his oratorical skills to stir up the passions of an ignorant and violent mob[12]), the modern critical tradition stems from mid-twentieth-century attempts to understand the totalitarianism of Hitler's Germany and Stalin's Russia. The role played by language in totalitarian regimes was explored by writers like George Orwell (most famously in his novel *Nineteen Eighty-Four*) and the German Jewish philologist Victor Klemperer, who wrote that 'Nazism permeated the flesh and blood of the people through single words, idioms and sentence structures which were imposed on them in a million repetitions and taken on board mechanically and unconsciously.'[13] More recent work in this tradition has examined the contribution made by language to what Edward S. Herman and Noam Chomsky called 'the manufacture of consent' in western democracies like the US,[14] the political uses of what the linguist George Lakoff calls 'framing',[15] the biases covertly embedded in the language of supposedly objective news reporting,[16] and the rhetorical strategies – including dogwhistling – used by modern political communicators.

I call this a 'tradition' because it is not a unified field of inquiry, but a set of loosely related projects pursued in a range of academic disciplines (as well as, in some cases, outside the academy). What those engaged in it have in common is a political commitment to social justice combined with the belief that language plays an active role in maintaining unjust social arrangements – from which it follows that language criticism can play a part in the struggle against injustice. If people are made aware of the linguistic techniques used by demagogues and propagandists they will be better able to resist their malign effects. This is not a new argument (Orwell and Klemperer made it too), but in the last decade it has taken on a new urgency.

What has prompted this upsurge of concern is the rapid and dramatic rise of right-wing populism and far-right extremism.

'Rapid and dramatic' is not an overstatement: at the beginning of the twenty-first century few people would have predicted that populist 'strongman' leaders would soon come to power on almost every continent, and that far-right parties (some direct descendants of twentieth-century fascism, others more recent creations which recycle its obsessions) would be represented in the legislatures – and in some cases the governments – of democracies all over Europe.[17] Nor would many have foreseen in 2001, the year of 9/11, that twenty years later the security services in western countries (including the US) would be as worried about white nationalist terrorism as they were about the Islamist variety. Even in 2016, when Donald Trump was elected US president (itself an event that took many by surprise), no one imagined that four years later he would refuse to accept electoral defeat, that his supporters would attempt to seize the Capitol by force, and that another four years after that he would win a second presidential term. Until recently such things were the stuff of dystopian fiction; now they are political realities.

The rise of populism has also brought some noticeable changes in political language. Whereas old-school racists and social conservatives turned to dogwhistling as a way of appealing to prejudice while maintaining some semblance of linguistic decorum, a lot of the new populists' rhetoric is anything but decorous. It's a confusing mixture of strategies like dogwhistling, which disguise the speaker's real message, and strategies which do exactly the opposite. Donald Trump habitually makes public statements which are openly and outrageously bigoted (like his claim in September 2024 that Haitians in Ohio were eating other people's pets), as well as blatantly false statements on all kinds of subjects (though politicians have always lied, they have generally made more effort to conceal it). He also embraces, at least obliquely, conspiracy theories which not long ago were so far beyond the bounds of 'respectable' political discourse that any politician who gave them credence would have been seen as unfit for office. Today's populist leaders have shown that relying on slurs, lies and conspiracy theories is no longer automatically a losing strategy. Though many Americans do deplore Trump's rhetoric, for others his language is part of his appeal: it sends the message that he is 'one of us', someone who is willing to say what 'they' don't want you to hear.

This is the context in which dogwhistling is now discussed, and in some ways it has changed the discussion. There is, for instance, more academic work which considers dogwhistling alongside and in relation to other rhetorical strategies used by right-wing populists.[18] But in other ways the discussion has not changed. It continues to treat language as a tool, or weapon, of the right, and to see the right's increasing extremism as the central issue for contemporary language criticism.

This book, as I said earlier, will take a different approach. Not because I don't think right-wing populism and extremism pose a serious threat to democracy and social justice: I do think so. Since Donald Trump re-entered the White House in January 2025 the gravity of that threat has become even more apparent. But I also think most contemporary language criticism paints a picture which is partial in both senses of the word. There is, I will argue, a more complicated story to be told about the politics of language in our time. In that story the rise of the far right is not the only significant recent change, and it isn't only on the right that we see authoritarian and manipulative linguistic tactics being deployed in the service of political goals. When I say this, I am not trying to downplay the threat posed by the right. My argument, rather, is that to counter that threat effectively, the right's opponents need to be willing to look at the whole picture, and to reflect on what some of their own linguistic practices may have contributed to the current state of play.

Another story? Populism, polarization and the culture wars

I began this chapter with my experience, or perception, of seeing references to dogwhistling more and more frequently in the news media and on social media. Once I'd noticed this, and started to look more closely at the references themselves, I saw some other things which got me thinking about their function – what they were for, as opposed to what they were about.

Many or most of these references were accusations (or in the news media, reports of accusations). In itself that's not surprising: when you call a message a dogwhistle you are always implicitly accusing whoever sent it of doing something morally culpable. What was more unexpected was that these accusations didn't always fit the template I mentioned earlier, in which the accuser speaks from a progressive standpoint and the accused is on the political right. Sometimes those positions were completely reversed.

In January 2024, when the Labour leader Keir Starmer said in the House of Commons that the then-prime minister Rishi Sunak didn't 'get Britain', Sunak's fellow-Conservatives immediately accused Starmer of dogwhistling, insinuating that the UK's first non-white prime minister was not really British. I found this interesting for two reasons. First, it's a striking case of the right appropriating both a concept (dogwhistling) and a political concern (racism) which is traditionally associated with the left. Second, in context it was clear that Starmer's point was not about Sunak's ethnicity or colour, but about his status as a multimillionaire, someone who didn't 'get' the concerns of ordinary Britons about rising living costs and collapsing public services because those things did not affect him.[19] It also seemed clear that the Conservatives who attacked Starmer knew that. They were using the charge of dogwhistling not because they really believed Starmer was a racist, but to divert attention from a criticism of Rishi Sunak which they believed would resonate with the public (opinion polls at the time showed that Sunak was widely regarded as aloof and out of touch). And their strategy was effective: in the subsequent media coverage the story was not 'Starmer criticizes out-of-touch prime minister', but 'Starmer accused of using dogwhistle tactics'.

Analyses of dogwhistling have always emphasized the political work dogwhistles do for speakers who use them. But what examples like this one show is that *accusations* of dogwhistling also do political work. They can be made strategically, to discredit an opponent or divert attention from the issue at hand. This works for some of the same reasons dogwhistling itself works; more exactly, perhaps, it exploits the way dogwhistles work. Because dogwhistles are designed to give the speaker plausible deniability, an accusation of dogwhistling is impossible to refute. It's useless for someone in Keir Starmer's position to protest that he didn't mean what he's accused of having meant: since that's exactly what he'd say if he had, in fact, been dogwhistling, the fact that he says it proves nothing. Of course, not everyone will believe he's guilty as charged; but like dogwhistles themselves, accusations of dogwhistling send a clear message to those who are predisposed to hear it.

The work that accusations of dogwhistling does may help to explain why a concept developed largely on the left, and prototypically used by progressives to attack conservatives, is now being deployed in a wider range of political arguments. Though it's still fairly unusual, at least in my observation, to see mainstream conservative politicians playing the dogwhistle card (perhaps because this will often leave them open to the charge of hypocrisy, along the lines of 'since when have you people cared about racism?'), it isn't unusual to see accusations being made against progressives by other progressives. In that context the charge of dogwhistling serves more than one purpose. As well as causing reputational damage to the individual being targeted, it makes clear to others in the same political community what counts as acceptable or unacceptable speech – and what will happen to them if they cross the line.

The commonness of these accusations is as much a sign of the political times as the rise of right-wing demagogues like Trump, but it isn't something I've seen discussed in the literature on dogwhistles. Maybe the authors prefer to concentrate on what they see as the most serious political threat, the one coming from the far right. As I've already said, I don't disagree with their assessment of that threat. But I do think that focusing exclusively on the right leaves out some other recent developments which are relevant for our understanding of the bigger political – and linguistic – picture.

One of those developments is an increase in political polarization. A widening gap between political parties has been observed by researchers in many countries.[20] In the US, for example, the Democrats and the Republicans – parties which were once criticized for being so similar that many voters struggled to distinguish them – have moved further and further apart. Polls conducted by NBC News, which has been asking respondents the same questions since 1989,[21] show that on many issues Republicans have moved substantially to the right. Thirty years ago almost as many Republicans (48 per cent) as Democrats (56 per cent) thought the government should restrict access to firearms; today only 22 per cent of Republicans think so. Democrats' views have also shifted, but in the opposite political direction. Between 2012 and 2022 the proportion of Democrats who described themselves as 'very liberal' rose from just under a fifth to nearly a third: nearly 90 per cent now believe abortion should be legal in all or most circumstances, and over 80 per cent support same-sex marriage. Less than twenty years ago those figures were 68 per cent and 40 per cent.

You may have noticed that the issues I've just mentioned – gun control, abortion, same-sex marriage – are all flashpoints in what are commonly referred to as the 'culture wars'.

What's distinctive about 'culture war' issues is their ability to divide people for reasons which have less to do with economic self-interest and more to do with identity and values. Those divisions may cut across traditional party lines: that was true, for instance, of British people's views on whether the UK should leave the European Union when a referendum on that question was held in 2016, and of the positions people in numerous countries took on measures such as lockdowns, vaccines and mask mandates during the peak phase of the Covid-19 pandemic. Both those issues generated high levels of what political scientists call 'affective polarization', a kind of antagonism with deep emotional roots: it arises from the combination of feeling a strong identification with one group and perceiving other groups as a threat to your identity and way of life. It's this kind of polarization that has increased most markedly in recent years. And while the reasons are doubtless multiple and complex, one contributory factor is the emergence of new political movements which have deliberately set out to intensify it.

The populist right is a case in point. Unlike the previously dominant strain of ('neoliberal') conservatism, whose main preoccupations are economic, and which often takes a more relaxed approach to social issues (in Britain it was a Conservative government that legalized same-sex marriage, while simultaneously pursuing a punitive programme of economic austerity), the populist right has made culture wars central to its political project. This was a conscious decision, reflecting the belief of right-wing 'gurus' like Andrew Breitbart (who died in 2012) and Steve Bannon (who would later become Trump's chief strategist) that 'politics is downstream from culture', or in other words that a shift in the prevailing culture is a necessary precondition for any radical political change. They believed that the left had been winning the cultural battle since the 1960s, entrenching liberal social attitudes as the norm – and not only because (as conservatives had complained for years) liberals dominated key cultural institutions like the mainstream news media and Hollywood, but also because the left paid more attention to storytelling and had better, more engaging stories. According to this theory, the right needed to develop its own, equally powerful narratives. That prompted the populists to lean heavily on issues like race, immigration, sex and gender, which could be used to tell a story in which traditional (white, male, Christian, patriotic) identities and ways of life were threatened by powerful forces. As we saw on 6 January 2021, that story has resonated sufficiently with some people to make them willing to take drastic political action.

The turn to culture, however, has not been as one-sided as is sometimes claimed. Leftists often maintain that culture war is a right-wing tactic, designed to distract people from serious problems like racism, economic inequality and the destruction of the planet and instead channel their anxieties into conspiracy theories about vaccines or moral panics about gender-neutral toilets.[22] But while it's true that the most explicit recent advocates of this tactic have been right-wing populists, the idea that the left does not engage in culture wars – or that it only does so under provocation from the right – does not stand up to scrutiny. The left has a long tradition of treating cultural questions as politically non-trivial.[23] And today it has its own internal version of the culture wars, which arises from a conflict between more traditional forms of progressive politics and the newer current which is popularly labelled 'woke'.[24]

'Woke' is, of course, a highly contested term, and is often used in ways that are both derogatory and all-encompassing: if your only information came from the right-wing press you might think anything remotely progressive was 'woke'. Recently, however, critics of 'wokeness' who are themselves liberals or leftists have made a more considered attempt to explain what distinguishes this strain of thought and activism from other progressive currents.[25] The main point these critics make is that the 'woke' left has adopted an ultra-radical form of identity politics (the making of political claims by and for groups defined by attributes such as their race/ethnicity or sex/gender) which is at odds with the liberal/leftist tradition of universalism. 'Wokeism' accords more importance to the specific identities that make groups or individuals different than to what they have in common by virtue of their shared humanity (or for old-school Marxists, their shared position in the class system under capitalism), and rejects the idea that there are rights, values or forms of knowledge which transcend identity-based differences.

But contributors to this literature make two other criticisms which are particularly relevant to the subject of this book. One is that the 'woke' left pays disproportionate attention to language. Yascha Mounk, a self-described liberal, observes that 'in virtually every developed democracy activists now expend enormous efforts on changing the way in which ordinary people speak'.[26] A more radical leftist critic, Frederik DeBoer, concurs: contemporary social justice movements, he says, have 'an obsessive focus on using the right language'.[27] DeBoer is one of several writers who have related this obsession to 'elite capture', the fact that progressive political movements are now dominated by highly educated and privileged people such as students at elite universities and high-status professionals who work with words, ideas and information.[28] Their preoccupation with language, critics argue, has more to do with its centrality to their own lives than with its relevance to the concerns of the actually marginalized. Some also suggest that it's a product of despair: faced with the ascent of the right, and with the failure of recent protest movements like Occupy, #MeToo and Black Lives Matter to lead to radical and lasting change, the left has retreated into what DeBoer describes as the 'rabbit hole of language policing and linguistic politics'.[29]

This reference to language policing brings us to the second criticism, which is about the tactics used by 'woke' activists to silence and discredit opponents. These include not only online callouts, pile-ons and mobbings, but also offline campaigns to 'cancel' individuals by disrupting events where they are speaking, threatening to boycott outlets which publish their writing, making complaints to their employers with the intention of getting them fired, and (in legal jurisdictions that permit it) reporting them to the police for alleged hate crimes. Critics accuse the activists who use these tactics of turning their backs on the liberal/leftist tradition which believes in open political debate and regards freedom of expression as a core progressive value.

That's a charge many activists would not deny. Some consider the very phrase 'free speech' (sometimes scornfully rendered as 'freeze peach') to be no more than 'a dogwhistle for the alt-right'.[30] When their critics point out that some of their tactics were pioneered in alt-right culture war campaigns like Gamergate, a sustained campaign of harassment targeting feminists in the videogame industry,[31] they typically respond with some version of the argument that the ends justify the means. Whereas the Gamergaters were misogynists and trolls whose attacks on feminists served no higher moral purpose, the 'woke' target people who are guilty of engaging in hate speech – an intervention they say is justified by the harm hate speech causes to marginalized groups. *Harm* is a keyword in this argument: the importance of words and symbols in 'woke' activism reflects not only the general importance accorded to those things by educated elites, but also the more specific view (one with obvious antecedents in the tradition of language criticism I discussed earlier) that 'symbolic violence' is as harmful as the physical variety.

Since the 2010s the question of what constitutes 'harmful' speech, and how democracies could or should regulate it, has itself become a culture war battleground. It has always divided opinion, but a contemporary Rip van Winkle waking from a twenty-year slumber might find today's divisions unfamiliar and confusing. While conservatives have continued their long-standing efforts to get books they disapprove of removed from school and public libraries (recent popular targets include children's books with LGBT themes and works of history or fiction dealing with race and racism),[32] they have now been joined by progressives campaigning to decommission or sanitize texts whose content or language they claim is harmful.[33] Today it is often conservative-led organizations that defend free speech against 'woke' legislators, publishers, universities and corporate DEI ('diversity, equity and inclusion') departments, while the liberal organizations which used to do that job – perhaps most notably the American Civil Liberties Union (ACLU), which once defended the right of Nazis to march through a Chicago suburb populated by large numbers of Jewish Holocaust survivors – are now reluctant to act for anyone whose speech or beliefs they regard as hateful.[34]

The law is also a front in this battle. In many parts of the English-speaking world, governments (typically of the centre-left) have either introduced or proposed to introduce legislation to regulate hateful speech. These provisions have attracted opposition not only from conservatives, but also from liberals and some leftists. In Scotland, a law making it a criminal offence to 'stir up hatred' against certain groups has been criticized for defining the offence so vaguely as to allow anyone with a personal or political grudge to report their target to the police, who will then be obliged to investigate. Apart from the individual injustices which might result, critics are worried about the chilling effect this could have on public discourse generally. Canada is currently considering a Bill which has prompted similar objections. In Australia and Ireland, proposals to strengthen current legal protections against hate speech (or as Australia calls it, 'vilification') have been modified or put on hold because of the controversy they generated, but in both cases the party responsible has said it hopes to bring forward stronger measures in future.[35]

Even in the US, where the First Amendment to the Constitution ('Congress shall make no law ... abridging the freedom of speech') precludes this kind of legislation, there have been suggestions that change may be needed. In a speech to the World Economic Forum in October 2024, the Democrat John Kerry, speaking in his capacity as Joe Biden's Special Presidential Envoy for Climate, observed that combating climate change was an especially challenging task in a democracy where a significant section of the public had been convinced that the problem either doesn't exist or has been deliberately created by the government. He went on: 'If people only go to one source and the source they go to is sick and ... has an agenda, and they're putting out disinformation, our First Amendment stands as a major block to our ability to just, you know, hammer it out of existence.'[36]

It is surely not unreasonable to ask how modern democracies should address modern problems like online disinformation, nor to suggest that a document written in the 1700s might not offer much helpful guidance (the Founding Fathers could not have foreseen the internet, just as they could not have foreseen the AK-47 when they affirmed Americans' right to bear arms). But any attempt to discuss such matters in good faith is now liable to founder on the rock of tribalism, a form of intense partisanship which leads each side to interpret the other's words and motivations as more extreme and more hostile than they really are.[37] On the right, Kerry's speech was taken as further evidence that a 'global elite' wants to control what ordinary people can say, think or believe. That response, in turn, confirmed the view of some leftists that free speech is a reactionary cause, and that anyone who argues for it while claiming to hold progressive views is either a dupe or a closet supporter of the far right.

When activists on both sides take such extreme and uncompromising positions, one effect is to deter many people who feel no strong allegiance to either tribe from getting involved in discussions of contentious issues. Those debates, they say, are 'toxic', and they fear the potential consequences of speaking up. But if the only people who do speak up are unrepresentative of the wider public, and more concerned about tribal loyalties than finding solutions to real-world problems, the discussion becomes unproductive as well as toxic, reducing complex questions to a series of simplistic debating points. In the case of free speech, for instance, all democracies impose some restrictions (e.g., on speech that directly incites violence). But disagreements which are really about where, how and by whom the lines should be drawn are constantly framed as if one side believed that anyone should be allowed to say anything in any situation, and the other proposed blanket state censorship.

The tendencies discussed in this section – polarization, tribalism and the increased salience of 'culture war' issues – are more than just a backdrop to the rise of dogwhistle politics. Disputes about the meanings of messages – more specifically, about whether they have hidden, hateful and harmful meanings which might justify censoring them and/or punishing whoever sent them – have become an increasingly visible and influential arena in which those tendencies, and the associated conflicts, play out.

In political settings, the question of what was 'really meant' by a disputed utterance (like Keir Starmer's assertion that Rishi Sunak 'doesn't get Britain') will usually remain unresolved. Since there is no higher authority to issue a definitive ruling, people are free to assess the competing interpretations and make up their own minds. But disputes about whether something someone said or wrote was a coded message of hate are now arising more frequently in other contexts – on social media platforms, in workplaces, on university campuses and at public meetings or demonstrations – where they are subject to formal adjudication by various authorities: administrators, HR managers, police officers, and ultimately, in a growing number of cases, tribunals or courts of law. In these cases a ruling does have to be made, and for the accused person the stakes are high: if the judgment goes against them they could lose their job, their reputation, and even, in some circumstances, their liberty.

This development doesn't only affect the individuals directly involved. The cases that get reported and discussed are only the most visible signs of a shift which affects society as a whole – not least because it generates so much conflict and resentment. When Donald Trump won the 2024 US presidential election, many commentators suggested that this result reflected not only widespread economic discontent, but also a growing hostility to the Democrats' perceived 'wokeness'. One of Trump's most attention-grabbing campaign messages tapped into this mood directly, using the line 'Kamala is for they/them. President Trump is for you.' Though the theme of the ad was a specific culture war issue (trans rights), the slogan also played on more general concerns about 'woke' language: it spoke to voters who, as one American I know put it, 'have had it up to here with people like us [i.e., educated, privileged and politically progressive] telling them what they can and can't say'.

Being critical of dogwhistle politics

There is a strongly held belief among politically engaged people that, as a popular hashtag expresses it, #LanguageMatters. That view is influential on both the left and the right: its best-known modern representative, George Orwell, is claimed by both (though the criticisms they cite Orwell in support of are different, following the rule that it's only ever your political opponents who are guilty of abusing language). But while I don't dispute that language matters, there is more to say, and indeed to know, about how much and in what ways it matters.

In this book I'll try to address those questions in a way that acknowledges their complexity.

Many claims about why and how much language matters are based on simple, common-sense assumptions. They are not informed by either a theoretical understanding of how linguistic communication works or evidence that certain ways of using language have the effects their critics assume – such as causing people to have false beliefs, making it impossible for them to think certain thoughts, inciting them to commit atrocities or traumatizing them in the way they might be traumatized by a physical assault. Now that these claims are being pondered in courtrooms and invoked by politicians as reasons to change the law, they are urgently in need of critical scrutiny. 'Critical', however, should not mean 'dismissive'. It is no more justifiable to treat contentious claims about language as axiomatically false than to treat them as self-evidently true. Rather we should examine the evidence that exists on (at least some of) the questions that cause contention. Though on its own that won't resolve conflicts which in the final analysis are political and moral, I'd like to think it might do something to make the arguments, and what's at stake in them, clearer.

What I've just said might sound as if I think I'm above the fray, a neutral arbiter of a conflict I have no stake in. But clearly I do have a stake in this discussion, and a perspective on it which will inevitably reflect my own experience, knowledge and political beliefs. Though I don't think that's a reason not to try to be even-handed, I do think that if you write about politics you should be transparent about your own.

So: the political perspective I write from is that of an old-school progressive. My primary commitment throughout my adult life has been to feminism: if you've heard of me you may know that I'm the author of several academic (and a couple of more popular) feminist books. In my younger days (the late 1970s and 1980s) I was a grassroots activist in what was then called the Women's Liberation Movement; during the

Thatcher/Reagan era I was also involved in leftist campaigns against hospital closures, nuclear weapons and 'Clause 28', a legal provision that made it an offence to 'promote homosexuality'. I got a lot of my early political education from leftists, some of whom were of the 'hard' or revolutionary variety, and though my own socialism is strictly democratic (as the child of working-class Tories I never thought revolution was on the cards, nor – to judge from what I knew about life in the Soviet bloc – that it would be an improvement), on many issues I find the position of the UK Labour Party (which for a while I belonged to, and still generally vote for) frustratingly un-radical.

Apart from general considerations of transparency, there's another reason for spelling this out which is connected to the tribalism I noted earlier. Anyone who questions certain progressive orthodoxies can now expect to be described, however inaccurately and implausibly, as having conservative or far-right sympathies. Since her views on sex and gender became a matter of public controversy, J. K. Rowling has been repeatedly accused of sympathizing with the US Christian right (a lobby which would like to ban her 'Satanic' Harry Potter books, and has on several occasions held public burnings of them); Salman Rushdie's robust statements in support of free speech have been said to reflect his 'privilege' (the privilege of an author who was forced to spend several years in hiding because religious fanatics wanted to kill him, and who ultimately lost an eye to one such fanatic). This is absurd, but it's where we are. That so many self-defined progressives cannot even acknowledge the existence of differing viewpoints within the progressive camp is one indication of how intolerant social justice politics has become.

The same tendencies are evident in progressive thinking and activism around language. Some might say that's nothing new: similar criticisms were made of the non-sexist language campaigns of the 1970s and 1980s, and (especially) the 'political correctness' movement of the early 1990s. In those cases, how-ever (both of which I have studied and written about[38]), the concerns expressed by critics were at odds with the facts on the ground. PC speech codes were a niche phenomenon, largely confined to some university campuses and (in Britain) left-wing local councils; many of the examples that inspired tabloid headlines about 'political correctness gone mad' were either unsubstantiated rumours (like the story that the Greater London Council had banned the supposedly racist term 'black coffee') or jokes (no one seriously advocated replacing *short* with *vertically challenged*). And as far as I was able to determine, at least in Britain, it was rare for compliance to be systematically enforced, or for breaches to lead to punitive sanctions.

Today the situation is different. Coercion and compulsion are playing a larger role than they did in earlier campaigns, and a much wider range of institutions are now involved – including, as I noted earlier, those that make and enforce the law. In a growing number of cases (some of which I'll discuss in Chapter 4) the language used by individuals is being aggres-sively policed – sometimes literally *by* the police – and the penalties for non-compliance can be draconian. The scope of language policing has also been extended. Whereas its targets in the 1990s were, with occasional exceptions, fairly clearly specified (many of them were offensive epithets whose use in workplaces or classrooms few people now would find accept-able), today communications which are not obviously offensive or uncivil may become candidates for policing on the grounds that they are dogwhistles, coded expressions of prohibited sentiments.

In the rest of this book I'll examine these developments and their consequences in more detail. As well as looking at a range of real-world cases, I'll draw on research evidence to assess the arguments which have been made on some of the key issues those cases raise – like how hate speech should be defined and regulated; what it means (and whether it's reasonable) to equate verbal with physical violence; and whether changing language is an effective tool for changing attitudes and behaviour. First, though, I'll look more closely at the ways of thinking about language and communication which underpin the claims I'll be discussing. I'll begin in the next chapter by considering how dogwhistles have been defined and analysed by academic experts.

2

Understanding Dogwhistles

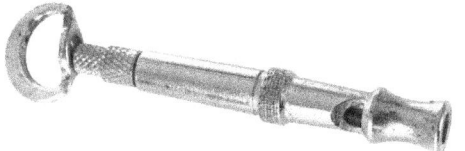

The last chapter defined dogwhistles in general terms; in this chapter I'll dig a bit deeper into the details, drawing on work done since the 1990s by academics who study them. I won't try to cover all of this literature, some of which deals with technical questions that are only really of interest to specialists. Rather I'll concentrate on what writers have had to say about the questions of most relevance to this book: how dogwhistles communicate, what effects they have on audiences, what role they play in modern politics and why that should concern us. I'll begin, though, with some more general points about the way linguistic communication works.

Saying, meaning and understanding

Humans are not endowed with the ability to read each other's minds. Though language is sometimes metaphorically compared with telepathy (described, for instance, as 'a window into the mind'), it does not give us direct access to others' mental processes. In that sense, imperfect understanding is our normal condition. We can never know everything another person knows, and we can never be certain that what we think they meant to communicate really is what they meant to communicate.

That doesn't mean, however, that we are doomed to spend our lives just talking past each other. In the absence of telepathy, our communicative superpower is our ability to reason from what someone said to what they meant, using not only our understanding of the words they utter, but also information that is not in the words themselves. What's said in so many words is never everything a hearer needs to know: it leaves gaps which we fill in using knowledge we already have. If someone says to me 'let's meet here again at the same time next week', I'll use my contextual knowledge about our present position in time and space to work out when and where they want to meet. If someone asks me for a drink of water I'll use my background knowledge about the world to work out that what they want is most likely a glass of water, not a teaspoonful or a gallon can. In cases like the ones I'll be discussing in this book, deciding what someone meant involves more complex calculations and leaves more room for uncertainty and disagreement. Yet in most situations we do manage to arrive at an understanding that, while it may not be perfect, is good enough to serve our purposes. How we do this is part of the subject matter of the academic discipline (usually counted as a branch of linguistics, though some of its foundational ideas were developed by philosophers) which is known as *pragmatics*. And since pragmatics is the source of a number of theoretical concepts which are relevant to the analysis of dogwhistling, it's worth taking a moment to look at a couple of its key ideas.

The first idea is the basis for what's called *speech act* theory: it's that utterances in a language don't just describe things in the world, they *do* things in the world. To understand what another person means to communicate, you need to work out not just what their words mean, but what action they are being used to perform. Sometimes the words spell that out. For instance, 'I bet you can't eat everything on your plate' is a bet, and 'we apologize for the inconvenience' is an apology. These examples belong to a class of utterances that the philosopher J. L. Austin called 'performatives', meaning that (so long as they are uttered in the appropriate conditions) the words themselves perform the action specified.[1] The person who says 'I bet you . . .' isn't reporting on a bet but making one: the bet comes into existence through the utterance of the words. But while all utterances do something, their linguistic form won't always tell you what. If a parent says to a teenager 'you're not going out wearing that, are you?' that might sound like (because linguistically it is) a question, but the parent expects the teenager to understand that in context it isn't a request for information, it's a request – or even a command – to go and change. If someone comes into my office and says 'it's cold in here', that sounds like a straightforward statement, but since people don't generally go around stating things at random I'll be likely to ask myself what else my visitor might be doing. Is she just making small talk, or is she hinting that she'd like me to turn up the heating?

The second idea originates in the work of the philosopher H. Paul Grice, who suggested that when we interact we observe, and assume others are observing, a 'Cooperative Principle' (CP), which he glossed as 'make your contribution such as is required, at the stage at which it occurs, by the accepted direction of the talk exchange'.[2] He then broke down this general requirement into a series of more specific 'maxims'. The first, which he called *quantity*, is 'give as much information as is required, and no more'; the second, *quality*, is 'do not say that which you believe to be false/do not have evidence for'; the third, *relevance*, is 'be relevant'; and the fourth, *manner*, is 'be perspicuous' (i.e., clear, as opposed to vague, rambling and obscure).

This principle helps to explain why I might reason that 'it's cold in here' is an indirect request to turn up the heating. On the assumption my visitor is being cooperative, I'll be asking myself why 'it's cold in here' would be a relevant and informative thing for her to say to me at that moment. Of course, my guess could be wrong: there's usually more than one relevant thing a speaker could be doing. It's also possible she isn't trying to be relevant or informative, but just talking for the sake of talking. Grice's argument wasn't that everyone always observes the CP (which is clearly not the case), but that treating cooperativeness as a baseline assumption enables us to reason more effectively about what other people are trying to tell us. He also pointed out that if cooperativeness is a baseline assumption, choosing *not* to be cooperative is potentially a meaningful act.

One of the examples Grice used to illustrate this was a (hypothetical) academic reference letter reading, in its entirety: 'Mr X's command of English is excellent, and his attendance at tutorials has been regular.' This is a clear violation of the CP: for the purpose a reference is meant to serve (helping the selectors to decide whether a job candidate is worth considering) it is insufficiently informative, and the information it does give is largely irrelevant. But that doesn't mean it communicates nothing useful. The letter's failure to 'give as much information as is required' is a clue, prompting the reader to look for some additional piece of information the writer might want to communicate without saying it directly. In this case the reader will be able to infer that the writer regards Mr X as unqualified for the position. Propositions which are communicated in this way – not by stating them upfront, but by prompting the recipient of a message to infer them – are called *implicatures*, and one of their properties is plausible deniability: if challenged later by an angry Mr X, the writer of the reference letter could assure him, quite truthfully, that the letter didn't say anything negative. That would, however, be disingenuous, since it would not acknowledge that what the letter said was different from what it communicated.

The imaginary reference letter is an example of a language-user acting in what you might call a 'cooperatively uncooperative' way. The letter does violate the CP, but it does so in a way that helps the reader: as a fellow-academic with the same expectations about what reference letters should contain, the reader can be expected to notice the violation and understand what it's intended to communicate. But there are other ways of violating the CP which are entirely uncooperative, because they're intended not to help but to deceive the recipient of the message. An obvious example is lying. Lying by definition violates the maxim of quality ('do not say that which you believe to be false'), but it can only achieve the liar's goal (passing a false statement off as the truth) if the recipient is not aware of the violation.

How dogwhistles communicate

Dogwhistles have something in common with Grice's imaginary reference letter, in that they too work by prompting message recipients to infer something that hasn't been stated directly. But they also have something in common with lies, whose effectiveness depends on being taken at face value. What explains this apparent contradiction is that dogwhistles are designed to communicate different things to different people. They are only intended to mean more than they ostensibly say to some members of the audience, not all. For the target group they contain a clue which enables an additional meaning to be inferred; people outside the target group, however, won't recognize it as a clue and will therefore take the message at face value. Those people are effectively being deceived. They aren't being actively lied to, but the dogwhistler is concealing something from them. How, though, do dogwhistlers pull off this trick – using exactly the same words to reveal a hidden meaning to some people while concealing that meaning from others? What kinds of words will be recognized as clues by the target group while having no significance for anyone else?

One answer to that question is 'codewords', words (or other signs) whose coded meaning is only known to members of a certain group. An example given by Jennifer Saul in her book *Dogwhistles and Figleaves* is the way contemporary far-right groups use the number 88 to signal Nazi sympathies: H is the eighth letter of the alphabet, so 88 = HH = Heil Hitler.[3] If you're part of the in-group that uses this code, you'll be able to read the presence of 88 in a message as a clue to the sender's political beliefs. But if you don't know the code, 88 is just a number. Even if you notice that, say, someone's online handle is 'JohnSmith88', or that a street photo they've shared includes a sign reading '88th Street', you'll have no reason to suspect the number has a hidden political significance. Saul labels this kind of message an *overt code* dogwhistle. That might seem like a confusing term – dogwhistles, after all, are by definition messages designed to communicate something they don't overtly say – but what Saul means by 'overt' (as opposed to *covert* – I'll come to what that means shortly) is a coded message whose meaning is unambiguous so long as the recipient knows the code.

This kind of coded messaging is not the exclusive province of political extremists. It can be employed in any situation where some members of the audience have knowledge others don't. This knowledge doesn't have to be as arcane as '88 = Heil Hitler': what works as a code depends on who the in-group is and what out-group(s) they are trying to exclude. The philosopher Anne Quaranto tells us, for instance, that in some US hospitals staff who need security back-up to deal with a violent or disruptive patient use the code 'paging Dr Strong' to summon help via the public address system without alarming other patients or visitors.[4] When adults spell words out to prevent young children from understanding them, they are using written language as an in-group code. Though we don't usually call examples like these dogwhistles, they work in the same way as the overt code type.

What Jennifer Saul calls *covert effect* dogwhistles, however, work in a different way – less like secret passwords and more like the effect noticed by opinion pollsters in the 1980s. As we saw in Chapter 1, the pollsters discovered that small variations in wording (e.g., *pretty happy* versus *fairly happy*) had a measurable effect on people's responses to questions, but the people this affected had no idea they were being influenced by the poll-designers' linguistic choices. A covert effect political dogwhistle, similarly, is one which influences people without their conscious awareness.

The effectiveness of political messages which appeal to bias in this covert way is the subject of one of the most influential studies of dogwhistling ever published, Tali Mendelberg's 2001 book *The Race Card* (though Mendelberg didn't use the word *dogwhistle*, which was not as common then as it has since become).[5] This book examines a case which is widely believed to have played a decisive role in the 1988 US presidential election, enabling (the elder) George Bush to overtake and ultimately defeat his opponent, Massachusetts governor Michael Dukakis. The Bush campaign ran a series of attack ads featuring a young black man named Willie Horton, a convicted murderer who had been temporarily released from prison as part of a weekend furlough scheme supported by Dukakis. While free, Horton had assaulted a white couple, raping the woman and stabbing her husband. Though in the US this incident (a violent crime where the perpetrator was black and the victims white) was always likely to be perceived as racially charged, both the ads and the media discussion they provoked avoided the subject of race entirely. There was no verbal reference to the fact that Horton was black – though his photo, which made that obvious, featured prominently.

This campaign proved to be highly effective. Bush had been lagging behind Dukakis in the polls, but the more attention the Willie Horton ads got, the more his support increased. Then, just before the election, the Democrat and veteran civil rights activist Jesse Jackson intervened. He accused the Republicans of playing the race card, exploiting the racist stereotype of black men as sexual predators who pose a threat to white women. This intervention made Willie Horton's race an explicit topic of discussion, and Bush's poll ratings immediately began to fall – though it was too late to save Dukakis from defeat.

For Mendelberg, the moral of this story wasn't just that racism wins votes. It was that racism wins most votes when no one is talking explicitly about race. As soon as, in her words, 'race went from subtext to text' thanks to Jesse Jackson's intervention, the spell was broken and the effect began to diminish. The more openly race was talked about, the less influence it had.

How can we explain this apparent paradox? Mendelberg's explanation focuses on the gap that exists in the post-civil rights US between the racial attitudes people profess explicitly and the ones they hold implicitly. Most white Americans by 1988 had explicitly embraced the 'norm of equality': they believed that racism was wrong, and did not want to be, or be seen as, racist. But subconsciously many were still holding onto the racist prejudices of the recent past. Mendelberg argued that such people will be more responsive to messages that appeal to racism implicitly than to messages which do so overtly. If a message is obviously racist, people who don't want to appear biased will consciously notice that and reject it. But implicitly racist messages like the Willie Horton ads can bypass this self-monitoring process.

In the Willie Horton ads it was a visual image (Horton's photo) that had this effect, but we have evidence from experimental studies that language can produce it too. Typically these studies have a two-stage design: first, subjects answer a set of questions used to measure racial bias, and then, at some later point, the same subjects are invited to answer a question on a topic to which racial bias could be relevant, though the question makes no explicit reference to race. Half of them are given a version of the question which includes a putative dogwhistle, while the other half get a version without the dogwhistle. The question is whether those who were exposed to the dogwhistle will give more biased answers than those who weren't.

One expression that's been investigated in this way is the phrase *inner city*. Particularly in the US, *inner city* has a history of being used to refer to neighbourhoods with largely black populations,[6] and over time it has become associated with a set of negative stereotypes of black people as, for instance, workshy, crime-prone and violent.[7] In 2017 the US political scientists Jon Hurwitz and Mark Peffley investigated whether its use influenced white subjects' responses to a question about prison policy.[8] The subjects were randomly divided into two groups: one group was asked if they supported spending more money on prisons to ensure that 'violent criminals' were locked up, while the other got a version of the question that referred to 'violent inner city criminals'. The researchers found that if you compared the responses of people who had shown similar levels of racial bias in the earlier test, the ones in the 'inner city' group displayed a stronger preference for more punitive prison policies. Studies using this method have identified other expressions which have this effect: for example, people who are asked if they're in favour of 'public assistance' or 'assistance to the poor' are more likely to give a positive answer than people who are asked if they're in favour of 'welfare'.

These experiments provide empirical evidence that the use or avoidance of a specific expression can induce a more or less biased response. It's not just that people have negative attitudes to whatever the dogwhistle term refers to: you don't get the same effect if you substitute a different expression referring to the same thing (e.g., *assistance* for *welfare* or *city centre* for *inner city*). But people vary in how susceptible they are to the influence of dogwhistles. In Hurwitz and Peffley's study those who'd shown higher levels of racial bias were also more affected by the wording of the question. This suggests that dogwhistle terms have what psychologists call a 'priming effect': hearing them makes a pre-existing bias more salient, so that it exerts a stronger influence on decision-making. But you can only make a bias more salient if it's already lurking in the background somewhere.

Of course, that doesn't mean dogwhistles are not a problem. Even if they don't create prejudice where none existed before, if they prime people to give more weight to their prejudices when making decisions then that's undoubtedly a cause for concern. For many critics, however, the problem with dog-whistles goes beyond their influence on susceptible individuals. The big issue, rather, is their malign effects on political culture: dogwhistles are seen as an insidious form of propaganda which is at odds with, and may pose a threat to, the norms of liberal democracy.

Dogwhistles as propaganda: the threat to democracy and the rise of extremism

Many writers on propaganda define it as a kind of communi-cation which seeks to manipulate its audience by appealing to emotions such as fear, anger and resentment rather than to reason, logic and evidence.[9] Modern propaganda, dissemi-nated most commonly via mass media, has been described as 'pseudocommunication'. It creates the impression that the producer of the message is engaging in the kind of rational, cooperative exchange described by theorists like Grice, but its resemblance to 'real' communication is largely illusory. Propagandists are uninterested in rational argument, and view the audiences they seek to influence more as dupes than as actual interlocutors. Propaganda thus flouts the fundamen-tal democratic principle that decisions should be based on informed deliberation in which every citizen has a voice.

According to the politics scholars Robert Goodin and Michael Saward, the use of dogwhistling in political campaigns is historically associated with the rise of mass media, which eventually put an end to the practice of 'whistlestop' cam-paigning, in which election candidates would travel around their patch (typically by train, hence the term 'whistlestop') giving each community they stopped in whatever message they thought it wanted to hear.[10] Since most voters had only local sources of information, they would never know if what a candidate had said to them was the opposite of what he'd told the people in the next town. With the advent of national (and later global) media this approach became increasingly untenable, but its goal – gaining support from constituencies with disparate interests – remained as relevant as ever to the business of winning elections. This gave politicians an incentive to embrace other communication techniques that allowed them to go on sending different messages to different constituencies.

Goodin and Saward argue that this way of communicating with the electorate creates a problem of legitimacy for whoever ultimately wins power. If a candidate's majority includes people who had totally different understandings of what they were voting for, the candidate, once in government, will have no clear mandate for any political programme. Whatever policies are then pursued in practice will be at odds with what some voters believe they were promised, and realizing they were deceived by deliberately ambiguous messages will cause those people to lose trust in the democratic process. 'Dogwhistle politics', these scholars conclude, 'is . . . not merely morally tainted, but also fundamentally counterproductive'.

But the political landscape has changed considerably since that assessment was made in the early 2000s. More recent writers have been less concerned about the problems dogwhistling causes for conventional democratic politicians, and more concerned about the opportunities it offers to those who are more interested in subverting democratic norms. Dogwhistling, it is argued, enables right-wing populists to smuggle views which would previously have been regarded as unacceptable into mainstream political discourse, where they can potentially influence a much larger audience than more openly extremist groups can reach. Even if these dogwhistles are only picked up by people who are already receptive to far-right ideas, the effect will be to embolden those people, giving them a stronger sense that their beliefs are legitimate and that other 'normal' people share them. Over time this may lead to a larger-scale shift in ideas about what is or is not acceptable.

There are reasons to think that such a shift has already occurred. A number of recent studies have failed to replicate the earlier finding that implicitly racist messages prompt more biased responses than openly racist ones. In 2017 one group of researchers in the US conducted a series of experiments which found that subjects' racial attitudes had a 'large and stable' effect on their responses, regardless of whether the stimulus they were presented with was implicitly or explicitly racist. The researchers' explanation was not that the earlier studies which found a difference were flawed, but that openly racist attitudes and language had become less stigmatized since those studies were done. 'Many citizens', they commented, 'recognize racially hostile content in political communications, but are no longer angered or disturbed by it'.[11]

This hasn't only happened in the US. Back in 2005, the UK Conservative Party ran a series of election ads in which the dogwhistle-announcing tagline 'are you thinking what we're thinking?' appeared under a statement representing what ordinary voters were supposedly thinking about various election issues. One of these statements was 'it's not racist to put limits on immigration'. At the time this caused outrage (some billboards were defaced by painting over the word *not*), but in hindsight what's most striking about it is the explicit denial of racism. The campaign designers apparently believed that people would only admit to thinking what the Conservatives were thinking about immigration (that there should be less of it, or even none) if they were reassured that this didn't make them racists.

Eleven years later, when another Conservative government called a referendum on whether the UK should leave the European Union, the picture was very different. Right-wing populism had become a significant force in British politics, and its representatives did not shy away from using openly racist messages to underline their point that a vote to leave the EU was also a vote against immigration. One ad put out by the Brexit Party superimposed an image of its leader Nigel Farage on a photo (which turned out to have been taken in Slovenia, not Britain) of a long line of Syrian refugees: the caption read, in large, bright red all-caps, 'Breaking point'. Picturing visibly non-white and mainly Muslim refugees (whereas most EU citizens living in Britain were white European workers) and suggesting that Britain was at breaking point because of them was an obvious attempt to appeal to racism, and it was condemned by Leave campaigners in other parties. But if Farage saw this criticism coming (and it's hard to believe he didn't), he evidently wasn't deterred by it.

It should not be thought, however, that this increasing tolerance for openly racist political discourse has rendered subtler strategies like dogwhistling obsolete: they are still useful to, and (as we'll see later) still used by, the likes of Farage. Though populists initially build support by presenting themselves as outsiders to the 'political establishment', their longer-term goal is usually to move into the institutions where real power is exercised. To achieve that they need to broaden their support base by appealing to new groups of potential voters, but ideally without alienating their existing constituency. By moderating their language they can give mainstream audiences the impression that their views have become less extreme; by using dogwhistles they can reassure their original supporters that their views have not, in fact, changed. Some far-right politicians have talked openly about using this strategy. Nick Griffin, formerly the leader of the (now defunct) white supremacist British National Party, told an audience of US-based supporters in 2000 that under his leadership the party had cleaned up its language: its literature no longer talked about 'racial purity', for example, but instead used what he called 'saleable words' like 'identity'.[12] An explicitly racist expression with strong Nazi overtones had been swapped for a term with more progressive associations – but for those in the know, *identity* was a dog-whistle for the same fascist beliefs the party had always held. The most successful European far-right leaders, like Marine Le Pen in France and Giorgia Meloni in Italy, have also understood that making the far right mainstream and 'modern' requires a shift away from the kind of language people associate with the fascism of Hitler and Mussolini.

Not all scholars agree that dogwhistling is a threat to democracy. Some see it as a normal and inevitable feature of democratic politics, precisely because winning power in a democracy requires politicians to gain support from groups with diverse and not uncommonly conflicting interests. Using coded messages is an effective way to persuade each of these interest groups that a politician or a party 'speaks their language'. One writer who has made this argument, the political philosopher Demetris Tillyris, points out that dogwhistling as a rhetorical technique can serve a range of ideological purposes. Though most writers associate it with racist or right-wing ideologies, it can equally be used by more progressive politicians (he cites Barack Obama as an example) to make 'implicit appeals or pledges of solidarity to the historically excluded'.[13] Tillyris sees leftists' opposition to dogwhistling as a form of purism which works against their own interests: if they insist on what he calls 'a politics of uncontaminated candour', eschewing a technique which is more effective for coalition-building, they will not gain the power they need to achieve their political goals.

Propaganda, like *dogwhistle*, is a negatively loaded word, almost invariably applied to political messages from a source the speaker disapproves of. In the scholarly literature I've been discussing, whose authors in most cases lean left, the messages that are criticized as propaganda come overwhelmingly from the political right. But in reality, we might ask, is there any kind of political rhetoric that does not make use of the techniques of propaganda as defined by these leftist critics? The left certainly does not confine itself to making arguments that appeal to reason: progressive social movements have always used rhetoric that plays on people's fears (e.g., of dying in a nuclear war, or for want of affordable healthcare) and their anger about unjust and oppressive practices. Of course that doesn't mean there's no political or moral difference between the rhetoric of social justice activists and the rhetoric of right-wing populists. But what distinguishes them is not whether they make use of propaganda, it's what purposes and interests they use it to serve. Like Tillyris, I think there are good reasons to be wary of arguments about the threat posed to democracy by 'manipulative' techniques like dogwhistling which rely on the assumption that those techniques can only serve the interests of right-wing authoritarians.

Dogwhistles as hate speech: harm and culpability

The harmfulness of dogwhistling has also become a contentious issue in the debates on hate speech I mentioned in Chapter 1. Those who argue for stricter regulation maintain that marginalized groups are not harmed only by the most overtly hateful messages, such as threats and incitements to violence, which are already prohibited in many societies: regulation should also cover instances where the expression of hate is implicit. Sometimes this proposal is advanced using the argument that if veiled expressions of prejudice are tolerated that will encourage more overtly hostile ones, creating a climate in which members of marginalized groups are more likely to face serious abuse and violence. But it may also be argued that coded messages of hate are harmful in their own right: being made aware that people hate you, even if they cloak that sentiment in vague and ambiguous language, is a threat to your psychological safety and wellbeing. I'll save a fuller discussion of these arguments about harm (and what evidence can be marshalled for or against them) until later on in the book. But they also raise some more theoretical questions about how dogwhistles communicate, and to whom.

According to the classic definition, dogwhistles are messages whose objectionable secondary meaning is intended to be picked up by audience members who share the prejudice being appealed to. A racist dogwhistle is meant to be heard by racists, a homophobic dogwhistle is meant to be heard by homophobes, and so on. The argument that dogwhistles have directly harmful effects on members of marginalized groups takes a step beyond that definition, since it implies that those people must also be able to access the secondary meaning, and perhaps even that they are the dogwhistler's primary targets. That's clearly the implication, for instance, of an example I'll discuss further in Chapter 3: a tweet whose author identified a scarf worn by a politician as 'a BLATANT dogwhistle taunt to trans people'. Evidently this tweeter believed that the politician's main reason for wearing the scarf was not (as the classic account would suggest) to communicate her prejudice to others who shared it, but to 'taunt' its objects, trans people.

Though I am less certain than the tweeter that the scarf was meant as a taunt, I do share her belief that the targets of a prejudice are in most cases able to identify coded as well as overt expressions of it. If they were not, there would be no cases of coded messages, as opposed to overtly hostile ones, being called out or reported as hate speech by a member of the targeted group, whereas in reality there are many such cases. In fact it seems likely that the people a prejudice targets will be particularly sensitive to the subtler forms it can take. The point of dogwhistling isn't to conceal the speaker's prejudice from its targets, but rather to exploit the feature of plausible deniability which makes it more difficult for their objections to 'land'. If a suspected message of hate is not overt and unambiguous (like, say, a badge emblazoned with the words 'kill all trans people'), what the sender meant it to communicate will be open to dispute; in cases like the politician's scarf (which she could plausibly deny was meant to communicate anything) there is no way to know for certain whether the dogwhistle interpretation is correct.

Because of that, some analysts have argued that it's a mistake to get bogged down in arguments about the (ultimately unknowable) intentions with which a disputed message was sent. Instead they suggest that efforts to establish whether a message was a dogwhistle should focus on the effect it had on its recipients. While that effect might not have been intended – someone might, for instance, have used a certain term without realizing it was a racist codeword – they point out that this makes no difference to the way a message is received. If people heard it as racist then it communicated racism whether or not it was intended to do so. This argument is in line with the general principle that it's ultimately the recipient who decides what a message communicates. It's also in line with the progressive political principle that only members of oppressed groups can determine whether something is oppressive to them: it's not for others to tell them what they should or shouldn't feel insulted or attacked by. But it does not resolve the real-world problems at heart of this book.

Consider, for instance, a case Jennifer Saul uses to illustrate the argument about intentions versus effects. In 2022 a group of linguists wrote to the Linguistic Society of America (LSA) urging it to sever its ties with the bestselling author Steven Pinker, on the grounds that he had publicly expressed views that were at odds with the LSA's own policy statements.[14] One issue the letter raised was Pinker's use of the phrases 'urban crime' and 'urban violence': the writers noted that *urban*, like *inner city*, is a racist dogwhistle. Other LSA members, however – including some highly respected semanticists (experts on meaning) – defended Pinker, arguing that nothing in his statements suggested he had been trying to make a racist point. Saul takes issue with this defence, commenting that 'what Pinker was trying to do is just not relevant to whether he used a dog-whistle term or not'. Whether a term like *urban* or *inner city* is a dogwhistle, she says, is a question about its effects, which have been demonstrated by empirical studies like the experiments I mentioned earlier. To concede that point, she goes on, is not to say anything about Pinker's culpability. The two questions, 'is this term a dogwhistle' and 'should this speaker be censured for using it', are logically separate, and the answer to the first is 'not at all decisive' with respect to the second.[15]

The problem I have with this is that in real-world arguments about dogwhistles the two questions are never separate. Allegations of dogwhistling always imply culpability, and that's often (as it was in this case) the reason they are made. I might even go so far as to argue that culpability is implied by the very fact that the term *dogwhistle* is used. As I noted earlier, it isn't generally used in reference to coded messages like 'paging Dr Strong', which work in the same way as dogwhistles but are understood to be non-culpable because they are uttered with benign intentions (e.g., in this case, preventing panic). And yes, I did just use the I-word, because in real-world disputes about offensive messages it is commonly assumed that both the meaning of the message and whether its sender deserves to be censured depend primarily on what the sender's intentions were.[16]

In 2020 Emmanuel Cafferty, a utility company employee in California, was photographed in a company pick-up truck making what the photographer, who posted the image on social media, described as a 'white power' hand gesture. Though to most people the gesture in question (forming a circle with the thumb and index finger while extending the other three fingers) is better known as the 'OK' sign, it has been appropriated by some far-right groups to serve as, in Jennifer Saul's terms, an overt code dogwhistle. As the image spread online, the utility company was bombarded with calls demanding Cafferty's dismissal. Like many organizations at the time (shortly after the killing of George Floyd by a police officer in Minneapolis), the company was keen to demonstrate that it took racism seriously; it suspended Cafferty without pay, and a few days later he was fired. Bewildered and upset, he told the media he had not only not intended the gesture to have a racist meaning, he hadn't known until he was suspended that it could have a racist meaning. He also pointed out that as a non-white person (of mixed Latino and Irish ancestry) he had no reason to support white supremacism. Writing about the case for *The Atlantic*, Yascha Mounk uncovered other details, both about the original incident and the company's handling of it, which led him to conclude that Cafferty's own understanding of why the company fired him – 'some guy sent a Twitter mob after them and they were just trying to defend themselves' – was probably correct.[17] The guy in question had already had second thoughts, telling a reporter he might have 'gotten spun up' and misinterpreted what he saw. But when Mounk asked the company if it had any other evidence against Cafferty, they refused to answer.

The extensive commentary this case generated is a good illustration of the point that real-life disputes about offensive messages tend to revolve around the question of intentions. No one (at least that I saw) disputed that people who took the gesture to mean 'white power' had been offended, angered and distressed; but the question that preoccupied most comment-ers was still whether Cafferty had intended to be racist. This is not, arguably, a sign of faulty reasoning, but just the same logic we ordinarily apply to communicative acts. The question we are always trying to answer in our interactions with others (which we understand to be exchanges with particular people, not with abstract symbolic systems) is not what the message itself means, but what the sender of the message means *by* it; and the way we approach that question is shaped in fundamen-tal ways by the assumption that communication is intentional behaviour.

In cases of alleged hate speech, however, it has been argued that this way of reasoning has the unjust effect of favouring the perceptions of the accused speaker – often a member of a more powerful or privileged group – over the perceptions of the people hate speech harms. If speakers can deny intending harm and on that basis be absolved of any responsibility for the effect their words had on others, those others suffer a double injury: first they are harmed by the speech itself, then they are harmed when their reaction to that speech is in effect dismissed as an overreaction, a taking of offence where none was meant. Such dismissals also reinforce the societal tendency to define hate speech in a way that systematically underestimates its prevalence and seriousness, again to the detriment of those it harms. If hate speech is equated only with the most extreme cases (those which express hate so overtly that it cannot plausibly be denied), most of the problem as minorities experience it will continue to go unacknowledged and unaddressed.

I agree that this is a problem, but what to do about it is a difficult question (a point I'll explore further in Chapter 4). Analysts who argue that the identification of coded hate speech should give more weight to effects and less to intentions have not, in general, given detailed consideration to what that would mean in practical terms for institutions tasked with adjudicating disputes. They might say that such questions, being more about the judgment of culpability than the explication of what and how messages mean, lie outside their remit. But as I've just said, I don't think those issues are so easily separated. And when a growing number of disputes are being dealt with by institutions, while more and more governments are legislating on the issue, the practical questions are getting harder to put aside.

Dogwhistles in context

The argument that some terms just are, objectively and invariably, dogwhistles tends to rely on examples where the putative dogwhistle is a single word like *welfare* or a fixed expression like *inner city*. It is harder to apply to cases involving either longer stretches of discourse or non-verbal symbols like photographs. But it could be argued that words don't have fixed, context-independent meanings either, and that analysts have underestimated the extent to which, as the French leftist Simon Assoun puts it, 'something *becomes* a dogwhistle depending on the situation in which it is enunciated, who is speaking, to what audience, or in what political moment'.[18]

When he made this observation Assoun was talking about a controversy that broke out in France in 2021, after the radical leftist politician Jean-Luc Mélenchon declared that 'the enemy is not the Muslim, it is the financier'. His critics immediately identified this as an antisemitic dogwhistle, using the word *financier* to evoke the stereotype of the wealthy Jewish banker, historically a staple figure in antisemitic propaganda. His supporters, however, maintained that he was using the figure of the financier/banker to make the orthodox leftist argument that the real enemy of the working class is capitalism. At a time when France's Muslims were under attack, he was saying that ordinary people should resist attempts by the ruling class to divide them along racial or religious lines. Assoun believed that the charge of antisemitism was a deliberate attempt to smear Mélenchon which gained traction because of the commonsense assumption that 'once a dogwhistle, always a dogwhistle'. If *financier* had ever been used by anyone as a code for antisemitism then that must also have been how Mélenchon was using it. That is not, Assoun was arguing, how language and discourse work.

Sociolinguists would agree that the meanings of words are not fixed and invariant: what they mean and how they function can vary significantly across contexts and communities. Some claims about dogwhistle terms are unconvincing because they take no account of that variation. The claim that the term *[biological] sex* is 'a dogwhistle for trans exclusion', for instance,[19] is more credible in relation to political discourse than scientific discourse, where the reasons for using the word – and indeed for talking about biological sex – are different. *Urban*, the term that was at issue in the Steven Pinker case, is frequently used in ways that cannot plausibly be read as dogwhistling (e.g., in an announcement I've just seen about a research project comparing rural and urban dialects in Denmark). Word meaning also changes over time: terms which function as dogwhistles today may not always have done so, making it unreasonable to charge everyone who has ever used them with dogwhistling. But you might ask, what about the experimental evidence that in present-day usage some terms do consistently activate biases (at least among subjects who already have them)? Couldn't *financier* be that kind of term? The short answer is yes (though the hypothesis would need to be tested), but that doesn't entirely negate Assoun's point, because experimental findings also need to be considered in context.

Experiments both have a context (they are conducted in a particular time, place and culture) and construct a context for participants – one which is in many ways untypical of the world beyond the lab. Since the researchers' aim is to investigate how subjects' responses are affected by a specific variable (like the way a question is worded), they must deliberately try to exclude other variables that would be likely to influence them in more 'ordinary' situations. One thing that's excluded in experiments like the ones discussed earlier is the influence of group dynamics. Each individual subject must answer the question independently, so researchers can be sure they're responding to the variable being tested, and not just being swayed by the opinions of other participants. But what's behind this precaution is the knowledge that in most social situations it is normal for the views expressed by others in a group to have an influence on the views we express ourselves: the desire to fit in and be accepted by our peers is a powerful motivator of human behaviour. That doesn't mean the effect observed in the lab isn't 'real', but it does remind us that in other circumstances it might be overridden, or rendered less significant, by other factors.

In political groups there is a particular kind of pressure to fit in: an individual's willingness to support the collective view may be seen as a test of their loyalty, both to the other people in the group and to the cause it exists to serve. This complicates the assessment of something like the leftist defence of Jean-Luc Mélenchon. It's not hard to imagine a member of Mélenchon's party feeling that his statement presents her with a dilemma. As a committed leftist she agrees with him that, at a moment when France is facing the most serious threat from the far right since the Second World War, it's imperative to present a united front – but she also thinks his use of *financier* was at best ill-judged and insensitive, and at worst a deliberate provocation. Should she voice her concern, or should she join her colleagues in defending Mélenchon from accusations which they all understand will benefit the right? The more polarized the conflict, and the more beleaguered the group, the greater the pressure will be to choose the second option. Claiming *not* to have heard a dogwhistle, therefore – just like claiming you did hear a dogwhistle – may be a strategic move in a larger political game. This is another illustration of Assoun's point that messages 'become' dogwhistles under certain contextual conditions – and whether they are heard as dogwhistles may depend as much on the baggage listeners bring to a message as on the characteristics of the message itself.

A dogwhistle by any other name?

Earlier I pointed out that some coded messages which work in the same way as dogwhistles, like 'paging Dr Strong', are not usually referred to as dogwhistles, at least partly because they are accorded a different moral status. The label *dogwhistle* implies not only that the message is intended to deceive (which is also true of 'paging Dr Strong'), but also that the deception serves a morally culpable purpose. If it is done for reasons people consider morally justified, the use of coded messages (like the telling of white lies) may be accepted or even applauded. And in politics the judgment of what is justified and what is culpable is affected, unsurprisingly, by tribal loyalties.

When President Donald Trump first took office in January 2017, he immediately embroiled himself in a bizarre public argument about the number of people who had turned out to celebrate his inauguration. Despite what appeared to be clear photographic evidence that the crowd was much smaller than it had been for his predecessor Barack Obama, Trump insisted that it had been larger. That claim was then repeated by the White House press secretary Sean Spicer, and when Spicer was accused of lying, Trump's spokeswoman Kellyanne Conway defended him, saying he had merely offered some 'alternative facts'. This Orwellian-sounding phrase caused an outcry among Trump's political opponents; it also caught the attention of the social media team at Merriam-Webster, who responded by tweeting out the dictionary's definition of *fact* as 'a piece of information presented as having objective reality'.

Though it was not unusual for Merriam-Webster's Twitter account to feature words which had recently been in the news, this was widely interpreted as a political intervention – a pointed rebuke to the Trump administration for misusing language in defence of a lie. The tweet quickly became news itself, and it was praised by the left-leaning press around the world.

Britain's *Guardian* newspaper ran an article headed 'Who's taking the fight to Donald Trump? It's Dictionary Guy'. After describing Merriam-Webster's tweet as 'the definitive take-down' of 'alternative facts', the writer went on to commend the dictionary for defending the 'basic idea that words have non-negotiable meanings'. This was not, she declared, a 'partisan outburst'; it was 'merely the assertion of fact, disinterested as the sea, neutral as weather'.[20]

But the response was very different a year later, when the British activist Kellie-Jay Keen (aka 'Posie Parker') paid to display the dictionary definition of another common English word on a billboard in Liverpool: 'Woman. Noun. Adult human female'. Liverpool was the venue for that year's Labour Party conference, and the billboard was a protest against a proposal to change the law which at the time was supported by all the main political parties. The proposal was that individuals should have the right to change their legal sex by what was informally known as 'self-ID', meaning that an applicant would only need to sign a formal declaration of their wish to change their birth-registered sex.[21] Keen used exactly the same tactic – reproducing a dictionary definition – to make exactly the same point as Merriam-Webster's tweet, that you can't mess with the meanings of words. An 'alternative fact' is a lie, and someone who isn't an adult human female can't be a woman. But her intervention did not prompt admiring headlines in left-leaning newspapers. It was denounced as a transphobic dogwhistle and taken down, with apologies, by the company that owned the billboard.[22]

The billboard's message was, indisputably, a dogwhistle. In addition to its ostensible meaning ('the dictionary defines a woman as an adult human female'), which was accessible to everyone (though its relevance was obscure unless you'd fol-lowed the debate on self-ID, which in 2018 was not yet on most people's radar), it was designed to send a political mes-sage to the subset of viewers, including Labour conference delegates, who would recognize it as alluding to the self-ID controversy: 'males cannot be women, and the law should not be changed to say they can'. But Merriam-Webster's tweet was also a dogwhistle. In that case, too, the ostensible message ('the dictionary defines a fact as . . .') was irrelevant and redundant unless you recognized it as alluding to 'alternative facts'. And if you did recognize that allusion you would surely conclude that Merriam-Webster was, indeed, 'taking the fight to Donald Trump'. So far as I know, though, the tweet was not described by anyone as a dogwhistle. The writer of the *Guardian* article even denied that it was politically partisan. And though the billboard appealed to the same principle progressive commentators had praised Merriam-Webster for defending in the face of populist demagoguery ('words have non-negotiable meanings'), they did not defend that principle when it was used to advance an argument they viewed as transphobic. What they had treated as a self-evidently true and virtuous belief when it was invoked to make a point they approved of became self-evidently wrong and bigoted when it was used to make a point they deplored.

I should perhaps clarify that in my own view 'words have non-negotiable meanings' is a bad argument whoever uses it.[23] If you believe it to be a good one, however, you should surely believe it applies in all cases, not just the ones where applying it produces what you regard as the 'right' result. But that kind of inconsistency is not unusual. As I commented in Chapter 1, it's only ever the bad people in the opposing political tribe who are said to be abusing language. When your own tribe does the same things with words, either the similarity passes unremarked or else the end is taken to justify the means. ('Am I prejudiced against demagogues who get their lackeys to lie to the public? Of course! Isn't every right-thinking person?')

Partisanship is in general very noticeable in discussions of dogwhistling. Historically, as I noted in Chapter 1, this has been a mainly leftist preoccupation, and that's reflected in the way the term is used. For instance, only some forms of prejudice (e.g., racism, homophobia, transphobia, antisem-itism, Islamophobia) – are commonly named in phrases like 'a ___ dogwhistle' or 'a dogwhistle for ___'. Dictionary entries like those I looked at in Chapter 1 do not contain examples referring to communist or feminist dogwhistles;[24] the claim that *sex* is a dogwhistle for trans exclusion is not paralleled by claims that, say, *cis* is a dogwhistle for trans inclusion (there are plenty of complaints about *cis*, but they are not couched in the language of dogwhistling). Academic discussions also tend to equate dogwhistling unproblematically with the promotion of reactionary right-wing views. In much of the literature I've cited in this chapter, all the examples discussed come from right-wing sources.

Recently, however – especially in the last decade or so – the term *dogwhistle* has entered the vocabulary of more and more people who are neither academic experts on language nor deeply engaged in political activism. In the next chapter I'll consider how these 'ordinary' language-users talk about dogwhistling – and whether its increasingly widespread use is changing the way the term is understood.

The question I asked at the end of the last chapter – do 'ordinary' English speakers use *dogwhistle* in the same way as experts? – is not just random and unmotivated. When specialist terms are adopted by ordinary language-users they may undergo what's sometimes called 'semantic drift', a process whereby the meaning of a word becomes broader, looser and more variable from speaker to speaker. This is a consequence of the way linguistic knowledge is transmitted. Academics acquire the specialist terminology of their field through explicit instruction, as part of a structured process of professional socialization. As students they use the same textbooks containing the same standard definitions (and if they deviate from the accepted usage they'll be corrected); later they read the same specialist literature and exchange ideas at the same professional conferences. These conditions produce a high level of agreement on what key terms mean. But when the same terms are picked up by people outside the expert community the conditions are very different. Ordinary speakers don't usually learn new words through explicit instruction: often they come across them somewhere and work out what they mean from contextual clues. This makes it more likely that different people will understand the same term slightly differently, and that their mental definitions will be broader and vaguer than the expert one. Over time, as more and more people adopt a term (often modelling their own usage on the way they've heard other non-experts using it), its meaning in ordinary language may diverge significantly from the usage of experts.

A well-known example is the way psychiatric terms like *phobia* and *trauma* are used in everyday English, with meanings that bear little resemblance to their definitions in medical textbooks. Mental health professionals regularly complain that laypeople are misusing language, and trivializing serious

3

Dogwhistles Everywhere: How the Concept Has Evolved

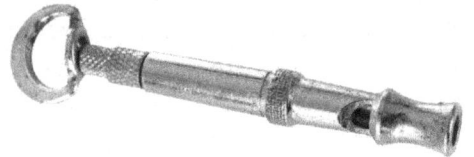

problems, when they call any strong dislike a *phobia* (in modern psychiatry the term denotes a class of severe anxiety disorders) and describe any vaguely stressful experience as *traumatic*. But these complaints are largely futile, since, as the philosopher Ludwig Wittgenstein famously observed, 'the meaning of a word is its use in the language'. If enough people use a term in a way that deviates from the supposedly 'correct' definition, what they use it to mean becomes its meaning. Among themselves the experts can maintain the codified definition, but they can't control the way words are used in the wider speech community.

Expert definitions may also change over time. *Trauma* is an example: according to the psychologist Nick Haslam, it's one of a number of terms used in psychology – others he discusses include *abuse, addiction, bullying* and *prejudice* – whose 'official' definitions have changed significantly since the 1980s. Haslam argues that this isn't just a case of 'drift', which suggests an aimless or directionless process. Rather it displays a consistent pattern whereby 'concepts that refer to the negative aspects of human experience and behavior have expanded their meanings so that they now encompass a much broader range of phenomena'.[1] In the past, for instance, the clinical definition of post-traumatic stress required the precipitating event to be outside the normal range of human experience (e.g., combat or natural disaster): it specifically excluded experiences like bereavement which almost everyone will face at some point. Today those exclusions have been dropped. The expert definition of *abuse*, a term that used to refer to repeated physical or sexual assaults, has broadened to encompass emotional and verbal abuse. *Prejudice*, once a descriptor for the overtly hostile attitudes displayed by some people, is now frequently applied to implicit or unconscious biases which everyone is said to be affected by. *Addiction* is no longer equated exclusively with dependence on drugs or alcohol; *bullying* can mean a single incident of victimization rather than a systematic pattern.

Each of these concepts has been 'stretched' to include both new forms of the original phenomenon (e.g., emotional abuse, cyberbullying, phone addiction) and less serious or less obvious instances of it. For Haslam the consistency of this pattern, which he labels 'concept creep', suggests an underlying cultural cause: he believes it reflects the 'ever-increasing sensitivity to harm' which has gone along with the adoption of a 'liberal moral agenda' in western societies over the last half-century.

Dogwhistle, the term whose evolution I'll be examining in this chapter, names a political rather than a psychological concept. But as we saw in Chapter 2, recent discussions of dogwhistling have had a tendency to emphasize its harmful psychological effects. That's an issue I'll address more directly in Chapter 5; in this chapter I'm mainly interested in exploring how the term is used today, and whether mainstream usage has 'drifted' from the earlier expert definition. But as I delve into those questions, it's worth bearing in mind the possibility that *dogwhistle* might also be an example of 'concept creep', and that current understandings of what it means and why it matters reflect, among other things, the 'increasing sensitivity to harm' which Nick Haslam identifies in other cases.

Before we get to what *dogwhistle* means, though, and whether that's different for different groups of users, we should take a closer look at how, when and why it stopped being a term used mainly by academic and professional experts, and became part of the political vocabulary of a much larger section of the population.

The mainstreaming of *dogwhistle*

One easily accessible tool for investigating word-use over time is Google's Ngram Viewer, which supplies year-by-year information about the frequency with which specific words or combinations of words appear in the texts that make up the

Google Books database. In the case of *dogwhistle*, the Ngram Viewer shows that its frequency has increased significantly since the beginning of the twenty-first century. Between 2000 and 2012 it rises steadily; in 2013 there's a large jump, followed by another steady but much steeper rise – between 2013 and 2019 the line on the graph is almost vertical. But while this is evidence of a general upward trend, if we want to dig into the details a better place to look might be the news media, which are often the main channel through which specialist terms are introduced and explained to a wider public – usually in reports or commentary on events to which those terms are relevant. It was in media reporting on the Covid pandemic, for instance, that many non-experts first encountered technical terms like 'herd immunity'. It's reasonable to think that political reporting may have played a similar role in popularizing *dogwhistle*.

With that in mind, I searched for the various forms of the word (*dogwhistle, dogwhistles, dogwhistled, dogwhistling* – along with their two-word and hyphenated variants) in a database of newspaper articles.[2] My search covered the period from the mid-1990s (when dictionaries tell us the term was first used in newspapers) to the autumn of 2024. The results confirm that *dogwhistle* has acquired transnational currency: they include items from English-language newspapers published in Australia, Canada, India, Ireland, Israel, New Zealand, the UK and the US. The internal composition of the sample for each of these places is also in line with the view that *dogwhistle* has acquired mainstream currency. In the subsample for the UK, for instance, where the newspaper market is segmented both by social class/education and by political allegiance, there are items from every national newspaper, as well as from several regional or local titles. Evidently the term *dogwhistle* is familiar not only to the left-leaning, university-educated professionals who read the *Guardian*, but also to the conservative, working-class and lower-middle-class readers of the *Sun* and the *Daily Mail*.

That, however, is a relatively recent development. The earliest examples in the database suggest that writers who used the term *dogwhistle* in the 1990s did not expect all their readers to be familiar with it: they often include a brief explanation of what it means, and outside the US it is sometimes identified explicitly as an American expression. A 1997 article in *The Australian* has both these features. Discussing recent statements on indigenous land rights made by Australia's then-prime minister John Howard, the writer accuses Howard of 'engaging . . . in what the Americans have called dogwhistle politics: the words are intended to be inoffensive to the naked ear; but there is a high-pitched message for those who want to hear it'. It is not until the early 2010s that the term begins to appear more regularly and without parenthetical explanations – most commonly in discussions of either white racism or anti-immigrant prejudice (which had become a major issue in Europe, including in the UK[3]) – and the real tipping point comes in the second half of the decade, which saw a sharp rise in the frequency of *dogwhistle*. That higher rate of usage has been maintained in the 2020s.[4]

What was behind the increase? Probably more than one thing, but there is one development that stands out: the global rise of right-wing populism. Between 2010 and 2019 right-wing populist leaders came to power in Brazil, Hungary, India, the Philippines, Poland, Turkey, the UK and the US, while right-wing populist parties gained increasing support and influence in a number of Western European countries. This made populism and populist rhetoric an increasingly salient topic for the news media as the decade wore on. In the UK its salience was boosted by two events that took place within a few months of each other in 2016: the referendum which led to Britain leaving the European Union and the election of Donald Trump as US president.

In some parts of the press these events were viewed as a worrying demonstration not only of how far the populist right had progressed, but also of how seriously most commentators had underestimated it: the consensus had been that Britain would vote to remain in Europe while Trump would lose to Hillary Clinton. One consequence was an outpouring of commentary which attempted to explain what had happened. While much of this writing concentrated on economic and social factors, there was also some discussion of the contribution made by the populists' communication tactics. Figures like Trump's chief strategist Steve Bannon and the British Brexit 'guru' Dominic Cummings were portrayed as masters of the art of using language to manipulate and misdirect, whether through coded messages like dogwhistles, mantra-like slogans ('Make America Great Again!' 'Take Back Control!') or apparently factual claims that were, and were easily shown to be, blatant falsehoods. Any questioning of these messages was decried as an attempt by 'elites' to frustrate the will of the people: in the US, criticism of Trump was dismissed as 'fake news', while in Britain doubts about Brexit were dubbed 'Project Fear'. Though there was nothing novel about the observation that politicians use language to manipulate and mislead, to many critics the populists' tactics felt new, extreme and deeply disorienting.

This was the context in which not only *dogwhistle* but a whole cluster of terms relating to the new populist rhetoric started to appear more regularly in public discourse. In 2016 Oxford Dictionaries declared 'post-truth' its word of the year (WOTY), while a year later Collins chose 'fake news'. Words of the year are selected partly on the basis of frequency (Collins noted that the frequency of 'fake news' in its corpus had increased by 365 per cent between 2016 and 2017) and the number of online searches they generate, but also because of a more subjective perception that they capture the year's prevailing mood or its most important trends. Many WOTY selections around this time (the 2016 and 2017 shortlists also included *alt-right*, *antifa*, *echo chamber*, *paranoid*, *populism* and *woke*) pointed to two related trends: increasingly sharp political divisions, and a growing tendency for people on different sides of the divide to inhabit different discursive worlds, staying in their own political echo chambers and treating anything said or written by the 'other' side as suspect. Whether or not they used the term, people (or more exactly, politically engaged people, especially on the anti-populist left) were developing the habit of actively listening for dogwhistles.

That habit has persisted. Since 2020 the overall frequency of *dogwhistle* in the newspaper database has remained fairly stable, but the range of topics which elicit references to dogwhistling has expanded. There is still a strong focus on racism, but there are more mentions of antisemitism and Islamophobia, and many more references to homophobia and transphobia. As in the 2010s, this can be related to what political issues received extensive media coverage during the relevant time period. But at a more general level, the significance of dogwhistling as an idea (or an accusation) since 2016 reflects the polarized culture of suspicion and distrust that developed in the Trump/Brexit era.

It might also reflect something else: the phenomenon of 'semantic drift' which I mentioned earlier. If mainstream users of *dogwhistle* define the term in a different way from experts, and if as a result they describe a broader range of messages as dogwhistles, we might expect to see an increase in the frequency with which the term is used – not because dogwhistling is objectively any more common than it used to be, but because of a change in people's understanding of what counts as dogwhistling. At this point, then, I will turn to the question of how – that is, with what meaning – the term *dogwhistle* is used in contemporary mainstream sources.

Dogwhistle and semantic drift

To investigate mainstream uses of *dogwhistle*, between October 2023 and August 2024 I collected examples from a selection of newspapers, magazines, websites, online newsletters and social media posts (especially on X/Twitter, the most politically engaged of the popular platforms).[5] This was a deliberately unstructured approach: what I was aiming for was not a representative sample that could be used to make quantitative generalizations, but a sample varied enough to provide a snapshot of the range of ways in which the term is currently used.

I collected many examples of mainstream usage that diverged from the expert definition, but I want to emphasize from the outset that my purpose in discussing these is not to criticize ordinary language-users for using *dogwhistle* 'wrongly'. That would be at odds with the axiom quoted earlier, that 'the meaning of a word is its use in the language', and with the understanding that as words are used by more people in more contexts their meanings will 'naturally' evolve. I've put 'naturally' in scare quotes, though, because semantic change isn't quite like biological evolution, a matter of natural selection acting on random mutations. Especially in the case of political terms like *dogwhistle*, it is often a response to larger social and cultural shifts. I've already suggested that the political events of the 2010s played a key role in making *dogwhistle* fully mainstream; in the following discussion my focus will be on how its use has evolved in response to more recent developments.

I'll start, though, with a reminder of the 'standard' definition. Though they may disagree on points of detail, philosophers and linguists who study dogwhistles are broadly in agreement on their main defining features, which can be summarized as follows:

1. A dogwhistle is a message which has, in addition to its ostensible meaning, a hidden or less obvious secondary

meaning – typically appealing to a prejudice (e.g., racism)
or a political allegiance (e.g., fascism) whose open expression would attract widespread disapproval.
2. Because it isn't obvious, the secondary meaning has 'plausible deniability': the author of the message can maintain, if
challenged, that only the ostensible meaning was intended.
3. The secondary meaning is meant to be picked up by a subset
of the audience – people who share or are receptive to the
prejudice it communicates – while escaping the attention
of those who are not receptive.

Some non-expert usage of the word conforms exactly to this
definition. In July 2024, for instance, while speaking to a group
of black journalists, Donald Trump said of Kamala Harris (who
had just replaced Joe Biden as his opponent in the 2024 presidential election): 'she was Indian all the way, and then all of
a sudden she made a turn and she went, she became black'.
Though many people found this bizarre as well as offensive
(did Trump not understand that Harris is biracial, the child
of an Indian-born mother and a Jamaican-born father?), one
X-user explained it as a 'specific dog whistle' addressed to a
subset of black Americans who identify as 'ADOS' (American
descendants of slavery). This group campaigns for reparations
to be paid to people whose ancestors were enslaved and then
brought to the US, but not to the descendants of immigrants
like Harris's father. On this account Trump's remark was
designed to convey to ADOS-identified listeners that Harris
wasn't one of them and it was not in their interests to vote for
her. Whether or not that interpretation is correct (with Trump
you can never rule out the possibility that his bizarre and
offensive remarks aren't hiding anything more complicated,
they're just bizarre and offensive), the post uses *dogwhistle* in
the orthodox way, to mean a message with a coded meaning that only a subset of listeners will pick up. Most of my
mainstream examples, by contrast, suggest their producers are

operating with a definition which resembles the expert one but is not identical to it.

Keeping it simple: from coded messages to clarion calls

One element of the meaning of *dogwhistle* which is uniformly present in mainstream usage (in my sample, at least, there are no exceptions) is the understanding that dogwhistles are messages that express and appeal to prejudice. For some users that seems to be the whole of the definition: they use *dogwhistle* essentially as a synonym for 'racist' or 'bigoted'. For instance, my collection of examples includes a reposting of an old tweet accusing the US politician Ralph Nader of dogwhistling because he had referred to Barack Obama as an 'Uncle Tom'. We might agree that it is racist (or, at the very least, arrogant and entitled) for a white politician to make this criticism, but it isn't a dogwhistle by the expert definition. Since 'Uncle Tom' is a well-known and overtly derogatory label for a black person who condones or panders to white racism, 'Obama panders to white racism' was not a secondary, ambiguous and deniable meaning, but the ostensible meaning of Nader's utterance.

Similarly, in summer 2024, when Kamala Harris became the Democrats' nominee for the US presidency and her opponent Donald Trump named J. D. Vance as his running mate, there was a flurry of interest in some comments Vance had made in an interview three years earlier, when he had referred to Harris and other female politicians in her party as 'childless cat ladies'. A *New York Times* op-ed piece called that phrase 'an uninspired dog whistle'.[6] By 'uninspired' I assume the writer meant that it invokes a well-worn sexist stereotype of childless women as unnatural and anti-social. But in this case as in the 'Uncle Tom' one, the prejudice being expressed is not disguised: unlike, say, 'inner city', an apparently neutral phrase that primes hearers to retrieve a negative stereotype, 'childless cat ladies' *is* the stereotype. Its negative meaning is impossible to deny, and indeed Vance made no attempt to deny it.

In some cases it's the words speakers use that suggest they don't define a dogwhistle as a disguised or non-obvious expression of prejudice. In January 2024, for example, an X-user described a politician's scarf as a 'blatant dogwhistle taunt'. And in August 2024, when anti-immigrant riots broke out in England and Elon Musk posted on X that 'civil war is inevitable', an expert on extremism quoted by NBC News said of the post: '[it] is a white supremacist clarion call. It is a dog whistle.'[7] This phraseology is at odds with the expert understanding of a dogwhistle, which by definition is not 'blatant', and certainly not a 'clarion call' (the word *clarion* refers to a military trumpet which was designed to be heard above the din of the battlefield).

Broadening the scope: inexplicitness, implicature and incitement

At first glance many of my other examples looked like the ones I've just discussed. But on closer inspection I realized that their producers had not completely dispensed with the idea that dogwhistles disguise their prejudice to make it deniable. Rather they seemed to have expanded the concept of disguise to encompass any mode of expression which was not fully direct and explicit.

This helps to explain the contrasting reception of two utterances which caused controversy during the UK general election campaign in summer 2024 – both attacks on the then-prime minister Rishi Sunak by members of the far-right Reform UK party. In one case a canvasser for Reform was heard using the racist slur term 'P*ki' to refer to the prime minister. No one called that a dogwhistle; they simply called the canvasser a racist. In the other case, however, Nigel Farage, the leader of Reform UK, criticized the prime minister's decision to leave an event commemorating D-Day early by saying: 'he doesn't really care about our history, he doesn't really care – frankly – about our culture'. Farage was immediately accused of using 'dogwhistle tactics'.

Why did the term *dogwhistle* seem appropriate in this case? It can't be because the racist implications of Farage's remark were only accessible to hearers who were racists themselves. Anyone who heard the remark had to work out what was meant by the phrases '*our* history' and '*our* culture' – who was the 'we' that by definition included Farage, but excluded Sunak? – and the most obvious if not the only plausible answer was 'British people of native (i.e., white) ancestry'. There is no other respect in which Sunak differs significantly from Farage: both men were born in the UK, attended elite private schools in the south of England and went on to work in the financial sector before embarking on political careers. However, since Farage made no explicit reference to Sunak's ancestry or his skin colour, listeners did have to do some interpretive work, using their background knowledge that Sunak is the son of South Asian immigrants to infer what Farage left unstated – that he doesn't care about British history and culture because he is not fully and authentically British.

Is this reliance on hearers to infer an unstated racist proposition enough to make a message a dogwhistle? For many ordinary speakers the answer seems to be yes, and it isn't hard to understand their reasoning. But as I noted in Chapter 2, most messages exchanged by people in the real world rely to some extent on hearers' ability to infer propositions which have not been directly stated. Defining messages as dogwhistles solely on the grounds that they invite or require hearers to infer an unstated, prejudiced proposition will catch many cases which lack the key distinguishing features of a dogwhistle as defined by experts: non-obviousness and plausible deniability.

Farage did try to deny that his comments had been racist, claiming that he'd been criticizing Sunak's lack of understanding of ordinary British people's feelings, which reflected not his ethnicity but his wealth and privilege. But this denial lacked plausibility because it did not fit with the content of the original message (would Farage have suggested that the Duke of Westminster, who is even richer than Rishi Sunak, is not included in the national 'we'?). Though he communicated racism less directly than the canvasser who used a racist slur, it was arguably still too obvious for anyone who heard his comment to be genuinely in doubt about what he meant.

Soon after the election (which was decisively won by the Labour Party, but saw Reform gaining nearly 15 per cent of the national vote and winning five parliamentary seats), a knife attack on a group of girls aged six to eleven attending a dance class in the northern seaside town of Southport left three girls dead and several more people seriously injured. False claims that the attacker was a recently arrived Muslim illegal immigrant started to circulate online, triggering a wave of anti-immigrant 'protests' in cities and towns across the country. These so-called protests (in reality they were race riots in which the rioters were white racists) quickly descended into violence, directed not only against immigrants (e.g., refugees housed in local hotels, one of which a mob tried to burn down) but also against long-established British Muslim and other minority communities. In the first week of August these events were discussed extensively in the media and on social media, and one recurring theme in these discussions was the role of dogwhistling in provoking them. This post on X was typical: 'They're out of control. All that pent up racism thanks to the likes of Farage, Tice, Rees-Mogg, Patel, Braverman, etc. This is what dog whistle politics leads to.'

This writer was not alone in suggesting that the anger and hatred expressed by the rioters had been deliberately stoked up over a long period by supposedly 'respectable' public figures like the right-wing politicians named in the post. Many people felt it was unfair that while the rioters were (deservedly) being punished, in some cases with prison sentences, the politicians whose rhetoric had encouraged them were facing no such consequences; they remained free, as some commenters saw it, to fan the flames of the violence their dogwhistling had incited by making public statements that contained yet more dogwhistles. Another X-user said of Richard Tice MP, the deputy leader of Reform UK, that 'he condemns violence and attacks on the police. Nobody else. He could argue otherwise, but his phraseology is the dictionary definition of dog whistling.'

Others suggested that the rhetoric of right-wing politicians matched the dictionary definition of something else: 'stochastic terrorism'. According to the Wikipedia entry for that term, which was shared by numerous people on social media:[8]

> Stochastic terrorism is targeted political violence . . . instigated by hostile public rhetoric which is directed at a group or an individual. Unlike incitement to terrorism, stochastic terrorism is accomplished by using indirect, vague or coded language that allows the instigator to plausibly disclaim responsibility for the resulting violence.

The entry goes on to explain that 'indirect, vague and coded language' refers to 'dogwhistles, jokes, hints, and other subtext in statements which fall short of a criminal threshold for causation'. Inciting either terrorism or racial hatred is a criminal offence in the UK: one woman who posted 'blow the [Southport] Mosque up with the adults inside it' on Facebook received a fifteen-month prison sentence. But so long as you don't spell it out as unambiguously as she did it's unlikely an incitement charge will stick. If some random stranger watching your YouTube channel takes your vague insinuations about Muslims as a suggestion that he should bomb a Mosque, you can't be held legally responsible.

One example of coded language which commenters picked up on was the phrase 'legitimate concerns', which was used by various right-wing figures to suggest that even if the violence could not be condoned, the concerns that had provoked it were justified. Others drew attention to Nigel Farage's use of two rhetorical devices: the 'just asking questions' formula which is a staple of right-wing conspiracy theory discourse (in the wake of the Southport attack, when false rumours were circulating about the perpetrator, Farage made a video in which he questioned whether 'the truth is being withheld from us'), and the populist formula 'ordinary folk' (as in, 'the government has ignored the legitimate concerns of ordinary folk').

This formula had already attracted attention during the election campaign, when Farage deployed it in response to questions about the explicitly racist language used by some of his supporters. While he acknowledged that a few individuals had 'let us down' (presumably he meant those who had been heard using racist slurs), in most instances, he maintained, Reform members were just using the everyday language of 'ordinary folk' rather than 'mainstream political Oxbridge-speak'. A writer in the *Byline Times* commented: 'Faced with reprehensible behaviour from members of his party, Farage chose to sound a dog-whistle . . . subliminally saying, to those who wanted to hear it . . . [that] these Reform members were simply saying what other people are afraid to.'[9]

What seems to have happened in these cases is that *dogwhistle* was used as an umbrella term for all the forms of 'indirect, vague and coded' language that people held responsible – morally if not legally – for stirring up racial hatred and inciting violence. Most of the messages referred to, however, were not, strictly speaking, dogwhistles. Rather they were vague expressions like 'legitimate concerns'; insinuations like 'is the truth being withheld from us?', which uses a question to imply, without directly asserting, that the authorities are lying; or 'other subtexts' like Richard Tice's (alleged) response to questions about the riots, which is a textbook example of Gricean implicature:

JOURNALIST: Do you condemn the violence of the rioters in [name of town where it is known people have surrounded and tried to burn down a hotel housing refugees, threatened worshippers at a local Mosque and hurled bricks at the police].

TICE: I condemn the attacks on police officers.[10]

This response violates Grice's maxim of quantity ('give as much information as is required') by condemning only some of the violence we know has occurred. From that we can deduce the implicature 'I do not condemn the attacks on refugees and Muslims.'

Anyone can make that deduction using basic pragmatic principles. But different people might come to different conclusions about what exactly Tice meant his non-condemnation to convey. Maybe some of his followers concluded he was covertly sending them the message that they should carry on attacking refugees and Muslims – in which case his statement would be an indirect incitement addressed to a receptive minority of his audience. A similar analysis could be made of Elon Musk's comment that 'civil war is inevitable'. This appears to be just a statement of Musk's personal belief that conflict about immigration in Britain will escalate to all-out war; but could far-right extremists have thought he was exhorting them to make that happen? Was that how Musk wanted them to read it? The extremism expert whose 'clarion call' comment I quoted earlier seems to have thought so: he described this and similar statements made by Musk not as opinions or predictions but as *'calls* for civil war'.

Though the statements made by Tice, Musk and Farage during the riots do not exactly match the expert definition of a dogwhistle, it's not hard to see why many people found it logical to use that term. If you believed, as many did, that the rioting mobs had been spurred to action by politicians and other powerful influencers, you might well think there was something particularly apt about a term whose original inspiration was the human master using whistled commands to get his dogs to do his bidding.

The examples I've discussed in this section suggest that in mainstream usage the meaning of *dogwhistle* has been broadened to encompass a set of communication strategies which have various things in common with classic dogwhistles: they are similar both in their functions (expressing and appealing to prejudice, and potentially inciting direct enactments of it) and in their linguistic or pragmatic characteristics (they are inexplicit, indirect and vague, avoiding unambiguously bigoted language and often relying on the hearer to infer something that has not been directly stated). But although this understanding of dogwhistling has important things in common with the expert understanding, ordinary speakers often appear to disregard some of the distinctions experts make, for instance between the ostensible and the secondary meaning of a message; they also tend to equate – from an expert perspective rather simplistically – non-obviousness with indirectness (which need not make a message ambiguous or hard to understand – everyone understands that the 'right' reply to 'have you got the time?' is 'five past three', not 'yes, why do you ask?') and innocuousness simply with the avoidance of extremely offensive terms like racial slurs.

This kind of broadening accounts for many of the examples I found in the mainstream sources I examined. It's not surprising to find it in a case where a technical term has become more widely used, and it isn't hard to see the logic behind it. But I also found some mainstream uses of *dogwhistle* that suggested a different kind of reasoning – one that isn't so easy to explain.

Dogwhistle detectives: obscure allusions and suspicious symbols

Whereas many of the examples in the last section were messages whose appeal to prejudice was arguably too overt for them to count as dogwhistles, the examples in this section are cases where the opposite is true: the claim that a message is a dogwhistle depends on arguing that apparently unremarkable words, images or objects are really allusions to or symbols of an extreme and hateful ideology. This fits with the expert account of dogwhistles as disguised expressions of prejudice which are not meant to be accessible to everyone, but it raises some of the same questions academic critics have asked about that account. Are the dogwhistle detectives in these cases uncovering something less acute observers have missed, or are their own sensitivities and preconceptions leading them to find things that aren't really there?

That question divided opinion in a case Jennifer Saul discusses in her book *Dogwhistles and Figleaves*. In 2021, when the Conservative Party of Canada (CPC) adopted the slogan 'Canada's Recovery Plan will secure the future for you, your children and their children', some people on the Canadian left noticed what they thought was a suspicious resemblance to a white supremacist text known to insiders as 'The 14 Words' ('we must secure the existence of our people and a future for white children'). Not only did the CPC slogan contain some of the same vocabulary (*secure, future, children*), it too consisted of precisely fourteen words; it also contained exactly eighty-eight characters (another far-right code, as I explained in Chapter 2). On that basis the slogan was interpreted as a deliberate allusion to The 14 Words, intended to convey to far-right extremists that the CPC was sympathetic to their views. Saul agrees with that reading, commenting that the slogan was 'either a carefully constructed dog-whistle or a truly remarkable coincidence'.[11]

But many commentators at the time were sceptical. How credible, for example, was the claim that the resemblance between the slogan and The 14 Words was too close to be coincidental? Only three words appeared in both texts (leaving aside common function-words like *the* and *for* which there's a high probability of finding in any text), and none of them were words you'd be surprised to see in mainstream political messaging. The promise of a secure future appeals to voters of all persuasions, and perhaps especially to the (non-fascist) conservatives you might expect the CPC to target. It also seemed unlikely that the slogan's eighty-eight characters were a coded message for neo-Nazis. How many people who see a slogan on a billboard or a flier would think of stopping to count the characters?

Another dispute about whether something was an allusion, and therefore a dogwhistle, blew up on social media in the autumn of 2023, when photos of the climate activist Greta Thunberg attending an event in support of the Palestinians in Gaza showed a blue plushie octopus toy in the background. Some people denounced the toy as an antisemitic dogwhistle, noting that Nazi propaganda had used the image of an octopus with its tentacles sprawling across the globe to symbolize the supposedly grasping nature of the Jews and their alleged desire for world domination. Others, however, found that interpretation far-fetched, pointing out that people with autism (a group it is well known Thunberg belongs to) often use plushies to help them manage the effects of the condition. If that was the function of the octopus, they suggested, then it was not an allusion to anything. Eventually Thunberg made a statement in which she endorsed the second interpretation. She said she hadn't known the octopus had been used as an antisemitic symbol, and apologized to anyone her plushie had inadvertently offended.

This may have placated some critics, but it clearly cut no ice with others. That is not, of course, surprising: denials of dogwhistling are automatically suspect because dogwhistles are designed to be deniable. But what that means is that disputes about whether something was a dogwhistle are ultimately impossible to resolve. Since no one has access to Greta Thunberg's private thoughts, there is no way to know for certain what she did or didn't intend; though competing hypotheses can be rationally discussed, they can never be proved or disproved beyond all doubt. And if neither of the competing interpretations can be definitively ruled out, the argument will quickly reach an impasse.

But it's important to recognize that what produces this result is rarely if ever *just* a disagreement about the meaning of words and symbols: the underlying conflict is political. The dispute about the octopus was a proxy war, in which the side participants took was largely predictable from their position on the actual war in Gaza. Those who advanced the dogwhistle theory were defenders of Israel's actions; most of those who argued against it were critics of Israel. The octopus was only relevant because it appeared in this political context; had Thunberg taken it to a climate protest it would probably have passed without comment. But in the context of the debate on Gaza it could be used by Israel's supporters to cast doubt on the claim that opposition to the war was motivated purely by humanitarian concerns. That, in turn, made it equally important for Israel's critics to refute the dogwhistle theory.

Am I suggesting that the interpretation of the octopus as an antisemitic dogwhistle (or of the CPC slogan as a fascist dogwhistle) was cynical, promoted by people who didn't believe it themselves, but who saw how they could use it to their own political advantage? Not necessarily. I do think these accusations are sometimes made in bad faith, but among people who feel passionately about an issue it's also possible they are an effect of confirmation bias, the well-attested human tendency to give disproportionate weight to observations that confirm your pre-existing beliefs. If you're convinced that fascists are everywhere, or that all criticism of the Israeli government is at bottom motivated by antisemitism, you may be predisposed to seize on anything that seems to support that belief, and to treat counterarguments as inherently unpersuasive ('but it can't be just a coincidence that this slogan has 88 characters') or as further confirmation of what you suspect ('that's exactly what an antisemite would say'). To less invested observers, however, these arguments can seem tunnel-visioned, paranoid and circular.

The opening ceremony of the 2024 Paris Olympics included a tableau featuring drag queens which attracted a large number of complaints. Religious leaders complained that it mocked Christianity (it was widely though inaccurately interpreted as a parody of Leonardo's *Last Supper*); conservative pundits criticized it as an in-your-face display of 'wokeness'; other viewers regretted that French culture had been represented by something they found ugly and vulgar. But for some commenters it was self-evident that these complaints could not be taken at face value. Whatever they purported to be about, they were all really dogwhistles for homophobia and transphobia.

It's undeniable that criticisms of drag may reflect prejudice against gay and trans people, but it doesn't follow that any criticism of any drag performance must be an expression of that prejudice. In this case it's surely possible that what people explicitly said they were complaining about really was what they were complaining about. But in arguments about dogwhistles it's not uncommon for anyone who doubts that a message is deliberately appealing to a certain prejudice to be told not only that they're wrong, but that they're only denying the obvious because they share the prejudice in question. That immediately invalidates whatever point they're making by putting it in the category of 'just what a bigot would say'; it denies that people could disagree in good faith, and in effect defines a dogwhistle as any message someone believes to be a dogwhistle.

In this case the supposed dogwhistling of people who objected to the drag queen performance was inferred from the fact that they objected. But my collection of examples contains a number of cases where the reasoning is the other way round: the identification of a message as a dogwhistle (and sometimes even the identification of it as a message, i.e., an intentional act of communication) depends on, and is explicitly justified with reference to, the pre-existing conviction that its sender is a bigot.

In January 2024 an X-user posted a photo of Laura Pascal, the Labour Party candidate in an upcoming local council election, out canvassing in London wearing a large red rosette on her winter coat and a thick plaid scarf around her neck. The X-user commented:

> after Laura Pascal is called out for her 'gender critical' transphobia, she goes campaigning . . . wearing a purple white and green scarf as a BLATANT dogwhistle taunt to trans people. GC bigots use the suffragette colours as their 'brand' to try and hide their transphobia.

This raises the same question as Greta Thunberg's octopus: what was the purpose of the scarf? Was it meant to be a political message, or was it just worn to keep out the January chill? You wouldn't ask that question about the red rosette that indicates a candidate's affiliation to the Labour Party, nor about the green, white and purple 'Votes for Women' sashes worn by the suffragettes themselves; both are unambiguous political symbols. But what Pascal wore was just an ordinary item of clothing. Plaid, in any combination of colours, is a classic choice for scarves, and scarves, unlike rosettes and sashes, are unremarkable things to wear in winter. Even the intentional wearing of suffragette colours is not a reliable sign that the wearer holds gender critical beliefs. In Britain, suffragette iconography has long been used to symbolize a generic and by now uncontroversial idea of feminism or women's rights.[12] Today all kinds of mainstream outlets sell 'cosy' suffragette-themed merchandise – items like greeting cards, biscuit tins and tea towels – and this clearly doesn't just appeal to consumers who are politically active feminists. I'd guess that only a small fraction of these merch-buyers either profess gender critical feminism or know the suffragette colours are part of its 'brand'; the 'generic' feminist use of those colours is still more common than the GC one. The basis for identifying Laura Pascal's scarf as a dogwhistle, a coded message of transphobia, must therefore have been the X-user's pre-existing belief that Pascal was 'a GC bigot'.

I'm not suggesting that the X-user's interpretation of the scarf was unreasonable or illogical: whether or not it was actually correct (which is, as always, impossible to know for sure) it followed a logic we all use all the time. As I explained in the previous chapter, expert accounts often downplay the importance of speakers' intentions for determining whether something is a dogwhistle, but ordinary speakers generally do think intentions matter, and they also assume that what they already know about an individual (e.g., in this case, Laura Pascal's views on sex and gender) is a relevant source of evidence about their likely intentions. In our everyday dealings with others we operate on the assumption that they have stable identities, beliefs and personal characteristics which we can expect their behaviour to reflect, and we take it that their previous behaviour has some predictive value (e.g., we're more inclined to believe someone is lying if we know they've lied before). These common-sense assumptions are of course blunt instruments, which can, and often do, lead us astray: people aren't always predictable, our knowledge about them is only ever partial, and our assessments of their behaviour are liable to be affected by all kinds of preconceptions and biases. But in the absence of telepathy we make the best use we can of the resources available to us.

Signs of the times

Human communication is unavoidably imperfect, but the conditions in which we communicate can magnify its imperfections. I don't think it's a coincidence that almost all the examples discussed in the last section came from discussions or debates on social media. In an already highly polarized political climate, the way these platforms work tends to polarize discussion further. They encourage the formation of echo chambers where one view of the world is constantly reinforced while others are presented as alien and threatening; they create an economy of attention in which the most valuable currency is outrage; and they make it easier for users, shielded by distance and anonymity, to resort to bullying, abusing and threatening those they disagree with. It's hard to imagine conditions more conducive to suspicion, distrust and defensiveness.

In some politically engaged circles these conditions have encouraged the ultra-suspicious approach illustrated by the examples I've been discussing. That a message could contain a malign hidden meaning is not just a possibility to be borne in mind; at the extreme it becomes an assumption to be confirmed by actively looking for reasons to believe it, and actively resisting alternative interpretations. If other people can't see the hidden meaning you see, that just shows how cleverly it's been concealed; if the message-sender denies having malign intentions, that's exactly what someone with malign intentions would say. These familiar moves, and the resulting, unresolvable arguments, are signs of our polarized and hyper-mediated times.

So far I've stuck fairly closely to questions about dogwhistling itself – how it works, who uses it, how it's talked about in various contexts. But as I explained at the beginning of this book, for me 'dogwhistle politics' is more than just a way of doing politics that makes use of dogwhistling as a rhetorical strategy, or exploits accusations of dogwhistling for political

advantage. It's a way of doing and thinking about politics that accords enormous significance to words and symbols, and treats the dogwhistle – a coded message with a reprehensible hidden meaning – almost as a template for the way they work. All kinds of communications may be approached with suspicion, in the belief that even if they aren't dogwhistles they function like dogwhistles, concealing malign intentions behind an innocent façade.

In the second half of this book I'll be exploring the phenomenon of dogwhistle politics in this broader sense, by looking at some of the key beliefs and attitudes which underlie it, and which are visible not only in responses to dogwhistling as such, but also in the handling of other kinds of 'problematic' language use. In Chapter 5 I'll consider the beliefs about language and harm which are a core element of dogwhistle politics; in Chapter 6 I'll focus on a common criticism of the 'woke' left – that it is obsessed with changing the words people use, in the belief that this will change the world itself. The next chapter, however, will concentrate on something else that is very much a sign of the times: the weaponizing of accusations of offensive or hateful speech in campaigns against individuals, which has led to a growing number of disputes about the meanings of messages being played out not just on social media, but in workplaces, universities, police stations and courts of law.

4

'An Offence to Be Offensive': Dogwhistle Politics and the Policing of Speech

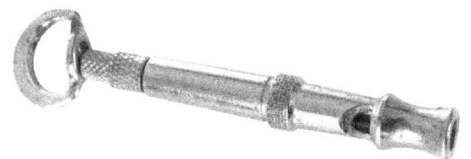

At the heart of dogwhistle politics as I conceptualize it in this book is an approach to language and communication which is not only suspicious and mistrustful, but also prescriptive and punitive. Just criticizing speech that offends you is not enough: it must be policed, prohibited and punished for the greater good. Not only has this become a common view among social justice activists, it has also made its way into the thinking of many mainstream institutions, including businesses, public services and branches of government. In this chapter I'll ask what's behind this development and what consequences it is having.

A point I want to emphasize is that its consequences are felt very widely: they don't just affect the powerful or those with strong political commitments. Whereas in most of the cases I've discussed so far the people accused of sending bigoted or hateful messages were high-profile public figures – national politicians like Nigel Farage and Jean-Luc Mélenchon, influential campaigners like Greta Thunberg and Kellie-Jay Keen, or individuals who were well known for other reasons, like Elon Musk and J. K. Rowling – in this chapter many of the stories I'll tell (and if I had space I could tell many more) are about ordinary people who found themselves in the firing line when something they said prompted a social media storm, a complaint to their employer or a report to the police. The pursuit of people like these is one indication of how pervasive the attitudes I'm examining have become. Another is the increasing involvement of powerful institutions, including the criminal justice system, in regulating speech and settling disputes about its meaning.

The new language police

In Chapter 2 I mentioned Emmanuel Cafferty, who lost his job at San Diego Gas & Electric after a photo of him making what was alleged to be a racist hand gesture was posted online in 2020. This was not an isolated case of what Yascha Mounk, writing in *The Atlantic*, called 'firing the innocent'. Mounk also drew attention to the case of a bakery owner who lost his business after someone found and publicized a series of racist messages his daughter, who was also his catering manager, had posted online some years earlier when she was a teenager. When her father became aware of this he fired her, but his suppliers still refused to do business with him and his landlord terminated his lease, making it impossible for him to continue trading.[1] Both these stories follow what has become a familiar trajectory. They begin with an individual being targeted on social media (usually for something they've said themselves, but sometimes, as in the bakery owner's case, because of their connection to the actual offender). Then, if the outrage generated online is not sufficient on its own to get a result, it may be followed up with offline actions – like calling a company to complain about an employee, or boycotting someone's business – which end with the target losing their livelihood.

All Mounk's stories come from the US, but similar things have happened elsewhere. Some of the most publicized British examples have involved writers, artists and academics. In 2019 the feminist artist Nina Edge was accused of transphobia by two art students on Twitter, and the controversy this prompted led John Moores University in Liverpool, where at the time she had a temporary teaching post, to cancel her contract without notice. In 2020 Gillian Philip, one of a team of authors contracted to produce children's books under the pseudonym 'Erin Hunter', was attacked by an online mob after tweeting in support of J. K. Rowling; within a day she had been told by the publisher of the Erin Hunter books that her services were no longer required.[2] And in a case I'll come back to later, at the beginning of 2022 the writer Kate Clanchy was dropped by her publisher after the language she had used in a book about teaching poetry to schoolchildren was denounced as racist on the popular review site Goodreads.

Other campaigns have targeted people in more mundane occupations. At one Cambridge college in 2020 a group of students demanded the dismissal of a porter: he was also an elected member of the city council, and when the students learned from the local press that he had voted against a motion on trans rights, they initiated a campaign to get him fired from his day job, saying that his presence in the college threatened the safety of trans students.[3] Also in 2020, a social worker was reported to her employer, Westminster Council, and to the body that regulates social work in England, by another social worker who alleged she had brought the profession into disrepute by sharing transphobic material on Facebook. Her employer suspended her on charges of gross misconduct, and the regulator initiated an investigation of her fitness to practise, putting her at risk not just of losing her job, but of being barred from any future employment. This is another case I'll return to: it ended with the social worker taking her employer and the regulator to an employment tribunal which found she had been treated unfairly.[4]

There were also cases where students pursued other students. In 2021 a law student at Abertay University in Dundee was reported by classmates for her 'offensive and discriminatory' views after she suggested during a seminar that a woman could be defined as 'someone with a vagina'.[5] Though in the end the university took no action against her, its investigation was not completed until after her final exams, which she was obliged to take while knowing that if the judgment went against her she would not be awarded her degree. In 2024 it emerged that a few years earlier an Exeter University student had been disciplined for saying that veganism was 'wrong' and gender fluidity was 'stupid' – not in class, or in any public forum, but during a phone call he made to a friend while alone in his own bedroom. He was overheard through the wall by the student in the next room, who promptly reported him to the university authorities. By his own account he was then visited by members of the campus night patrol, who told him 'you've been saying some very offensive things in here'. The subsequent disciplinary investigation ended with him being put on a 'behavioural contract': had he breached the terms he could have been expelled.[6]

In Britain it isn't just the campus patrol who might turn up at your door to accuse you of 'saying some very offensive things'. The title of this chapter alludes to a slogan, 'it's an offence to be offensive', which was used by Merseyside Police in a 2021 campaign to encourage the reporting of hate crimes. Though the slogan was withdrawn after critics pointed out that it misrepresented the law, it was indicative of a larger trend: police forces around the country have become very active in responding to complaints about offensive messages. In 2021 a Glasgow woman was charged with a criminal offence after tweeting a photo of a ribbon tied to a tree (the ribbon was said to be both a transphobic symbol – like the scarf mentioned in Chapter 3, it was white, green and purple – and a veiled threat of violence, on the grounds that it resembled a noose), only for the charges to be dropped when the case reached court.[7] In 2023 police in Yorkshire visited the home of a seventy-three-year-old woman who had been captured on CCTV taking a photograph of a sticker reading 'keep men out of women-only spaces' which someone had stuck on a 'Stand with Trans' poster that was displayed outside the town hall during Pride month. The woman insisted (and the police appeared to accept) that she had not been involved in making or putting up the sticker, and had not shown her photo of it to anyone except her partner. Nevertheless, she said the officers had told her she might be guilty of a hate crime.[8]

These are not, for the most part, cases of alleged dogwhistling. Though some of them did prompt dispute about what a message meant (was it reasonable, for instance, to interpret the ribbon as a threat?), in others that wasn't an issue: there is nothing ambiguous or coded about statements like 'veganism is wrong' or 'a woman is someone with a vagina'. The question in those cases was whether people's freedom to make such statements should be restricted, either by the law or by institutions like companies and universities. That has always been a contentious question, but recently the conflict has intensified.

The question is probably most contentious in relation to the expression of political opinions. The laws currently in force in the UK do make some forms of political speech unlawful (for instance, if they incite violence or are likely to cause serious public disorder), but the bar is supposed to be high because of the importance accorded in democracies to free speech and open debate. Freedom of expression (including the freedom to 'receive and impart information and ideas') is protected by the European Convention on Human Rights, to which the UK is a signatory. In addition, Britain's main anti-discrimination law, the Equality Act 2010, prohibits employers and service providers from discriminating against people because of their religious and philosophical beliefs. That applies both to what they do believe and what they don't: it's unlawful to discriminate against someone either because they are, say, a Catholic or because they are not a Catholic.

To qualify for protection under the Act beliefs must meet a number of criteria, which include being judged 'worthy of respect in a democratic society'. Not all beliefs pass that test, but a number of the cases mentioned above relate to one that has passed it: the 'gender critical' belief that men and women are defined by their sex, which is immutable, rather than their self-declared gender identity. Since the protected status of gender critical beliefs was established in a 2021 court judgment[9] it has in theory been unlawful for employers, universities or the police to take punitive action against people who express those beliefs (so long as the manner in which they do it does not involve threats or harassment, which are also unlawful). But in practice complaints about them have gone on being pursued. The cases mentioned earlier raise other questions too. For instance, should employers be able to discipline or fire people like the social worker and Gillian Philip for views they've expressed in a personal capacity? Arguably that infringes the right of employees, as citizens, to participate in political debates; but in the digital era more and more organizations have adopted policies regulating what employees can say online, citing their own right to protect their reputation. Gillian Philip's employer argued that her tweet supporting J. K. Rowling reflected negatively on everyone in the team that wrote the Erin Hunter books – though she had tweeted under her own name, not Erin Hunter's. Since 'Erin Hunter' was invented to conceal the fact that the books had multiple authors, and most readers probably had no idea who any of those authors were, it's hard to see how the views expressed by Philip-tweeting-as-Philip could have 'reflected on' anyone but herself. In the social work case, too, the posts which were alleged to have brought the profession into disrepute were shared on a private Facebook account that only about forty people could see. The tribunal criticized the employer and the regulator for taking no account of that fact.

Another question arises from the case of the student whose private phone conversation was overheard through the wall. The neighbour who reported him must have known the exchange was not intended to be overheard; was it reasonable for her to report it, or for the university to act on her com-plaint? There are circumstances in which most people would probably agree that a private conversation should be reported (e.g., if the participants appeared to be plotting a terrorist attack). But what the Exeter student heard was just a casual conversation whose content she found offensive. When I was a student nearly fifty years ago, reporting someone for that would have been not only impossible in practical terms (there was no official channel for such complaints), but also at odds with our social norms. The rule was basically 'live and let live', and if you really couldn't let something pass you had it out with whoever had offended you directly. We might wonder why that attitude has changed so radically – and not only in universities, but also in workplaces and in public life more generally. Why has making formal complaints about other people's language and opinions become such a common feature of institutional life?

One possible answer is, because we've become, as a society, more enlightened. It could be argued that the 'live and let live' attitude of the past was really just a shameful indifference to the bigotry and bullying some people had to deal with on a daily basis. If those people are no longer willing to put up with it, and if institutions have adopted policies which mean they don't have to, that's a sign things are moving – however slowly – in the right direction. Up to a point I'd agree: as someone who was young and female in the 1970s I'm certainly not nostalgic for the workplaces of the time, where bullying, harassment and all kinds of 'microaggressions' (not that they were called that then) flourished unchecked. Though these problems have not been eliminated by the policies in place today, on balance I'd still say it's better to have those policies than not to. But while more enlightened social attitudes have played some part in changing the way institutions deal with offensive speech, that change has also been driven by developments we might be less inclined to see as positive.

Changing institutional cultures:
'woke' capitalism, online activism and 'safetyism'

When Yascha Mounk pressed San Diego Gas & Electric to explain why they dismissed Emmanuel Cafferty, the company declined to give specific details, but they did give Mounk a general statement saying that 'SDG&E employees are held to a high standard and are expected to live up to our values every day, whether in interactions with fellow employees or the public.' The implication was that Cafferty had not lived up to the company's values. Although many people questioned whether that was a fair assessment in his case, what wasn't questioned was the general idea that ordinary workers doing ordinary jobs should be required not only to meet certain standards in their performance of the job itself, but also to demonstrate adherence to values prescribed by their employer. Today that idea is unremarkable, but it has only become so fairly recently.

In the late 1970s, when I too worked briefly for a utility company (the East Yorkshire Gas Board), there were no corporate values we were expected to 'live up to'. We were mainly expected to turn up on time and do what our supervisors told us. Any slacking, impertinence or obvious incompetence would earn a tongue-lashing (I once got one for drawing wonky lines on a map), but no one cared what our political views were or how we talked to each other in the office. The same was true of all the other organizations I worked for in the 1970s (a hospital, a high street bank and a pub). The people who ran these enterprises would have been baffled by the idea of adopting values beyond those which were obvious job requirements (e.g., honesty for bank employees). It would be another decade before organizations started to produce 'mission' and 'vision' statements explaining what they stood for in more general terms, and more than twenty years before it became common for companies to proclaim commitments to social justice or make public statements on political events which they were not directly involved in.

These practices, sometimes labelled 'woke capitalism'[10] (though the organizations involved aren't all capitalist – they also include charities and public institutions), have been criticized for appropriating progressive political causes, often in a very superficial way, for self-serving or cynical reasons (to enhance an organization's public image while distracting attention from its ongoing involvement in such 'unwoke' capitalist practices as avoiding tax and polluting the environment). But however shallow it may be, the desire of many organizations to appear progressive is something online activists can exploit in campaigns to get their political enemies disciplined or dismissed. One commonly used tactic is tweeting a criticism of someone and @ing the organization they work for so that someone in the organization will see both the criticism and any subsequent pile-on in support of it; another is publishing the email address of your target's boss online and urging your followers to make a formal complaint (sometimes the instigators of these campaigns even provide a link to a document containing a template).

This strategy is effective not only because social media make it easy to recruit large numbers of supporters, but also because organizations are receptive to it. Many have a policy of responding to all complaints, even if they come from people who have no connection with either the institution they're complaining to or the person they're complaining about. In some cases that policy has been imposed on them from above: when Abertay University's investigation of the law student mentioned earlier prompted questions about its policy on free speech, it explained that Scottish universities are legally required to investigate every complaint they receive from any source. In most cases, however, they have adopted it voluntarily in the belief that being accountable to the public is good PR and good for business.

But these policies make organizations vulnerable to being manipulated by activists who are not accountable to anyone. The colleague who complained about the social worker's Facebook posts, for instance, was an LGBTQ+ activist, and that was another reason given by the tribunal for finding the social worker had been unfairly treated. Her employer and the regulator had simply accepted the complainant's claim to be concerned about a colleague's professional conduct: they had made no attempt to check the complainant's own credentials, and in the light of that to consider the possibility that the complaint was politically motivated and malicious. The solicitor who represented the social worker at the tribunal called its judgment a warning to institutions 'that they must not let their processes be weaponised by activists'.[11] Since 2020 a number of other employers have lost similar cases, not uncommonly for similar reasons.[12] But activism-by-complaint has continued. Campaigners know that even if a complaint is ultimately dismissed, 'the process is the punishment'. Being investigated is time-consuming and stressful; few people who have been through the process would want to repeat it, and few people who've seen someone else go through it would want to be in that position themselves. If those people try to avoid becoming targets by keeping their heads down and their opinions to themselves, that too is a win for the activists.

Another explanation of what's changed is more controversial, but the claim has been made that formal complaints about other people's speech have become more common because many young people now struggle to deal with disagreements and conflicts which were once regarded as just a normal part of life. They exhibit what might be described as an extreme form of the 'increasing sensitivity to harm' noted by the psychologist Nick Haslam: having to engage with ideas they disapprove of, whether at work, in class or in social situations, causes them not just offence but severe emotional distress. Some seem to interpret any disagreement with their beliefs as an indication that others hate them and want to harm them; hence the now-common claim that the expression of certain views, or even just the presence of people known to hold those views, makes a campus or a workplace 'unsafe'.

Probably the most influential version of this argument was made by Greg Lukianoff and Jonathan Haidt in their 2018 book *The Coddling of the American Mind*.[13] These authors identify what they call 'safetyism' – meaning the belief that people should be protected from experiences and feelings that cause discomfort or distress – as an increasingly strong influence on the way many parents raise their children, and argue that children raised in this way do not develop the resilience they need to function as independent adults. One result is the kind of conflict that can now be seen on college campuses, where many students expect the college authorities to protect them in the same way their parents did. More conservative commentators have argued that the real problem is the 'victim culture' promoted in schools and colleges, as well as in much of popular culture. Today's young people have been indoctrinated, they say, into a worldview that makes victimhood a covetable status and encourages people to see victimization everywhere, so that any personal setback or minor slight is liable to be understood as an instance of it (I'll come back to these ideas in Chapter 5).[14]

But whatever we take to be behind it, I think it's clear that there has been a shift in the culture of many institutions. They've become simultaneously more politicized and less tolerant of political conflict, which is increasingly being dealt with using bureaucratic mechanisms like complaints procedures and policies specifying what the institution considers (un)acceptable. One consequence has been a proliferation of cases in which complaints about speech are investigated and adjudicated. In the next part of the chapter I'll look at a few examples, which I've chosen to illustrate some recurring problems with this way of managing political and linguistic conflicts.

Whose language is it anyway?

The dispute that led to Kate Clanchy's publisher refusing either to publish her future work or continue distributing her existing titles did not involve any formal adjudication. The business side of it presumably involved negotiations conducted behind closed doors; the political side involved a public debate conducted online and in the pages of various literary publications. But that debate raised an issue which has also arisen in cases that did involve formal judicial proceedings, and I will therefore take it as a starting point.

The book at the centre of the controversy was a memoir, *Some Kids I Taught and What They Taught Me*, about Clanchy's work teaching young people to write poetry at a state secondary school where a significant number of students had arrived in Britain as refugees, and were still adjusting to a new culture and language when they joined her class.[15] Her work with these students had been much admired: an anthology of their poetry had been published, and in 2020 her memoir had won the Orwell Prize for political writing. In 2021, however, a reviewer on Goodreads attacked the language used in some descriptions of the students – phrases like 'almond eyes' and 'chocolate coloured skin', which were criticized as racist or colonialist tropes. Those criticisms were then taken up by others, including some influential writers of colour who questioned whether *Some Kids* should have won an award. That, in turn, prompted other influential literary figures to come to the book's defence. An announcement that Clanchy would address her critics' concerns by rewriting parts of the text did not take the heat out of the debate. Some of her defenders protested that she shouldn't have to rewrite anything, while some of her detractors maintained that the book was beyond saving: it was, in one critic's words, 'riddled with racist and ableist tropes throughout' and contained language which was 'rooted in eugenics and phrenology'.[16] The writers of colour

who had criticized Clanchy also pointed out that their problem wasn't just with her, but with the white literary establishment which had uncritically celebrated her work: rewriting one book would not address that larger issue. Eventually the publisher, Picador, chose to part company with Clanchy (though *Some Kids* was later reissued by another publisher, Swift Press).

The summary I've just given suggests that this was a dispute pitting a white author, and the literary establishment that supported her, against readers and writers of colour who accused them of failing to notice what was obvious to anyone with lived experience of racism. But to frame it in those terms is to leave something out – the opinions of the refugee children (who by that time were no longer children) themselves. Did they think Clanchy was a colonialist 'white saviour' whose writing had done them 'unimaginable harm'? Some of them made it clear that they did not. One addressed the issue of language directly, saying: 'I am that girl with the almond eyes. I did not find it offensive.'[17] She went on to explain that in her (Hazara) culture of origin the phrase 'almond eyes' is 'a beautiful reference, widely used in our poetry and to proudly describe ourselves'.

This student's assessment of Clanchy's phraseology was no less informed by 'lived experience' than the assessment made by the critic who suggested it was 'rooted in eugenics and phrenology'. But the difference between the two judgments shows that there's a problem with trying to resolve disputes about the meaning and offensiveness of words by appealing to the authority of identity and personal experience. People who share an identity or an experience may nevertheless differ in both their political views and their ways of interpreting language. In cases where their interpretations conflict, the outcome will often depend (just as it does when identity isn't the central issue) on who, in a given context, has higher status, and is therefore accorded more authority.

The same issue arose in two recent British cases where the criminal justice system was called on to deal with a dispute

about language and racism. Both concerned the language used by non-white protesters criticizing non-white politicians. In one case a thirty-seven-year-old teacher was prosecuted for a racially aggravated public order offence. At a demonstration against the war in Gaza in November 2023 she had held a placard depicting two British Asian Conservative politicians (the then-prime minister Rishi Sunak and the former Home Secretary Suella Braverman) with coconuts around their heads.[18] *Coconut* is an expression used in UK minority communities to mean a person who is 'brown on the outside, white on the inside': to anyone who knew that, the placard was a coded message asserting that the politicians depicted were pandering to white racism by supporting Israel's actions. It came to the attention of the authorities when a photo of it was shared online by an anonymous right-wing account, which captioned the image 'it doesn't get more racist than this' and @ed London's Metropolitan Police (this tactic isn't only used by 'woke' leftists). However, at the trial the judge ruled that the placard was political satire rather than racist abuse, and the teacher was acquitted.

In the second case a twenty-four-year-old black man was charged with offences under the Malicious Communications Act, and stood trial in 2024; the proceedings ended with a jury acquitting him. On Twitter in 2022 he had taken issue with Ben Obese-Jecty, a black right-wing Conservative MP who had described concerns about the police shooting of an unarmed black man in London as 'hysterical'. During the online exchange that followed, the young man had tweeted a raccoon emoji, prompting the MP to report him to the police for racial abuse. Linguistically this is a slightly more complicated case, because the word the emoji was code for, *coon*, has a history of being used by white people as a racial slur akin to the N-word; when used within the UK black community, however, it has the same meaning as *coconut*. Obese-Jecty was well aware of that: he has written about the frequency with which he's been criticized by other black people using terms of this kind (*coon, coconut, House N----, Uncle Tom*),[19] and he appears to have a policy of reporting all such critics to the police. At one point he claimed on X that he had sixty complaints under active investigation.

There's no question that the terms Obese-Jecty objects to are – and are meant to be – offensive; there's also no question that they are racially specific, only usable against non-white targets. But it doesn't follow that they should be treated as no different from the racially specific abuse white racists direct against black people simply because they are black. As the British-Nigerian writer Nels Abbey commented, what's going on when *coconut* or *coon* is used by one black person to another is not racist hate speech, but 'an intra-communal political exchange, complete with intra-communal language, codes and mannerisms'.[20] Abbey argued that Obese-Jecty's strategy of systematically using the law against other black people had been enabled both by the (white-dominated) authorities' lack of understanding of the 'intracommunal code' and by their responsiveness to complaints from authority figures like MPs. But the result was that a law intended to protect minorities against racial hatred was in practice being used to protect powerful individuals from criticism, and to 'police political conversation within Black communities'.

These cases were another illustration of the point that 'the process is the punishment'. Though the two defendants were ultimately acquitted, being charged with a crime had serious consequences for both: the young man lost several job offers, while the teacher lost her actual job. Even police investigations which do not result in criminal charges may be sufficiently intimidating to deter people from expressing their opinions. This is one of the commonest objections to the laws which numerous democracies have introduced to deal with hate speech. At this point, then, we should take a closer look at how those laws are meant to work, and whether Nels Abbey's criticism of the way they work in practice applies to a wider range of cases.

Hate speech, hate crimes and hate incidents

I'll start with what the law says in England and Wales, where the cases just discussed were dealt with. It doesn't, in fact, say anything about 'hate speech', a term which has no legal status. 'Hate crime', however, does have a legal status. According to the Crown Prosecution Service (CPS) it means:

> [a] criminal offence which is perceived by the victim or any other person to be motivated by hostility or prejudice, based on a person's disability or perceived disability; race or perceived race; or religion or perceived religion; or sexual orientation or perceived sexual orientation or transgender identity or perceived transgender identity.[21]

If an offence is shown to have been motivated by 'hostility or prejudice' based on any of the characteristics listed, that may be treated as an aggravating factor, justifying a harsher punishment than the offender would otherwise receive. In most of these cases language is only relevant insofar as it provides evidence of the offender's motivation. If someone committed an assault while shouting racist or homophobic abuse, for instance, the abuse can be cited to argue that the assault (which is a criminal offence in all circumstances) was motivated by racism or homophobia. There are, however, some cases where what someone said or otherwise communicated may be an offence in its own right. For instance, the Public Order Act 1986 (which the teacher was charged under) includes provisions making it an offence to incite hatred on the basis of race, religion or sexual orientation by using threatening words (and in the case of racial hatred also 'insulting and abusive' ones).

There are also laws against racist chanting at football matches and against 'malicious communication' – sending indecent, grossly offensive or threatening messages to others through a public communication network (this was what the raccoon emoji tweeter was charged with).

In 2014 the College of Policing, a body which provides training and operational guidance to police forces, introduced a category of 'non-crime hate incidents' (NCHIs) – words and/ or actions which are perceived to have been motivated by hostility or prejudice, but which are not sufficiently serious to be investigated as actual crimes. If such incidents are reported the police record them, and the record, including the name of the person reported, is retained (supposedly only for intelligence purposes, but it may show up in the criminal record checks which are required for some kinds of employment). The recording of a NCHI can be done without informing the person concerned, but police officers also have the option of interviewing that person, telling them an incident has been recorded and advising them on their future conduct.

This system has become highly controversial. Recording allegations against someone on a police database, possibly without their knowledge, when there has been no investigation and no opportunity for them to contest the complainant's account, strikes many people as fundamentally unjust. There's also a widespread view that 'non-crimes', by definition, are not a matter for the police: officers should not be wasting time on trivial complaints about children calling each other names or people photographing stickers.[22] Civil libertarian groups have called repeatedly for NCHIs to be scrapped, and by the end of 2024 even the Chair of the College of Policing expressed concern that they had become a 'distraction', taking up time that would be better spent on other things and undermining public confidence in policing.[23] For the right-wing press, NCHIs have become a powerful symbol of 'woke' intolerance and authoritarianism. But it wasn't 'woke' activists who invented this approach: its foundations were laid nearly thirty years ago, by people at the heart of the British establishment.

As we saw in Chapter 2, some writers have argued that definitions of hate speech which emphasize the speaker's intentions over the effect a message has on its recipients serve the interests of the powerful and privileged, while giving insufficient weight to the perceptions of marginalized groups. That argument, which applies not just to speech but to hateful conduct in general, gained traction in Britain in the late 1990s, after the racist murder of the black teenager Stephen Lawrence by a group of young white men and the botched police investigation that followed. 'Botched', in fact, may give the officers involved too much credit, since they were not only incompetent and negligent but also clearly and shockingly biased: they disregarded the views of the Lawrence family and the wider black community, refused to accept that the killing had been racially motivated, and failed to act on credible information identifying those responsible. An official inquiry into the mishandling of the case, chaired by the retired high court judge Sir William Macpherson, concluded that the police were 'institutionally racist' and proposed a new definition of a racist incident as 'any incident which is perceived to be racist by the victim or any other person'. It was this victim-centred and perception-based definition that was subsequently adopted in guidance on hate crimes, and later hate incidents, more broadly.

That definition had been formulated with the best of intentions, and it was seen at the time as a necessary corrective to the bias exposed by the Lawrence inquiry. But more recently concern has grown that the principle is being abused: reporting people to the police, like complaining to their employers, has become a tactic used by political activists to silence and punish opponents. The way the police now respond to these reports also causes widespread unease. Whereas in the 1990s they were criticized for dismissing the concerns of community activists even in serious cases like the murder of Stephen Lawrence, today they are accused of pursuing trivial complaints and of taking sides in political arguments on contentious issues like trans rights and Israel/Palestine.

These concerns received some official acknowledgment in 2022 when Harry Miller, a businessman and former police officer, made a legal challenge to the College of Policing's NCHI guidance. Miller had had a NCHI recorded against him after complaints from activists that he had tweeted material which offended trans people. He was spoken to by a police officer who said he needed to 'check his thinking' and advised him not to tweet on the subject in future. His case ultimately went to the Court of Appeal, which found that the guidance the officer had been following was not compatible with the right to free expression as defined in the European Convention on Human Rights.[24] In 2023 new guidance was issued which stated that the police should avoid taking actions that were likely to have 'a chilling effect on free speech', and that officers should consider whether recording a hate incident was a 'proportionate' response to the behaviour reported. So far, however, this does not seem to have led to a significant decrease in the number of NCHIs recorded,[25] nor in the number of cases where the police have been accused of overreach and political bias.

But while the police have undoubtedly made some questionable decisions, they don't operate in a cultural vacuum. Their recent preoccupation with policing hate is clearly a response to the growth of concern about it in society at large, and it's also clear that their task has been complicated by the political polarization of the last decade. In 2024, when the Home Office asked the Inspectorate of Constabulary to investigate whether the police were fulfilling their obligation to be impartial when dealing with politically contested issues,[26] the inspectors were told by officers of every rank from PC to Chief Constable that they were constantly subjected to political pressure from local activist groups, community associations, elected councillors and MPs. They also felt pressure to respond to criticisms and comments made on social media. The inspectors concluded that while few officers were activists pursuing their own political agendas, many were susceptible to external pressure, confused about how to enforce the law impartially when opinions were so polarized, and struggling to keep up with changing requirements like the ones that resulted from Harry Miller's case.

The inspectors' report also suggested that concerns about the police not fully understanding the law (and sometimes misrepresenting it, as in 'it's an offence to be offensive') were not unwarranted: the training officers received was found to be variable in both quantity and quality, and one of the report's recommendations was that it should be improved. But we might also wonder if this uncertainty and confusion is exacerbated by the language used in anti-hate legislation.

Hate and the language of the law

The definition of a hate crime I quoted earlier is followed on the CPS website by a note: 'There is no legal definition of hostility so we use the everyday understanding of the word which includes ill-will, spite, contempt, prejudice, unfriendliness, antagonism, resentment and dislike.' What's being explained here is a very general principle: the words used in statutes are normally taken to have their 'ordinary' meanings, the same meanings they would have in everyday non-legal language. It's a common legal practice to use reference sources like dictionaries and thesauruses as evidence of what a word's 'ordinary meaning' is. This is what the CPS seems to have done: the last part of the note I've just quoted looks as if it has been lifted from the list of synonyms in an entry for *hostility*.

But if the purpose of the note is to help readers understand whether something someone said or did meets the criteria for being treated as a hate incident or a hate crime, then arguably this list is not very helpful. Though all the words on it could be substituted for *hostility* in some context or other, they are clearly not interchangeable with one another, since they denote quite different kinds and degrees of hostility. *Contempt* is much stronger than *unfriendliness*; *disliking* someone doesn't have to entail *resenting* them. Is the implication of the note that these various expressions of 'hostility' are all, legally speaking, on a par? Could someone have a hate incident recorded against them for saying they dislike lesbians, or for behaving in an unfriendly way to Christians? I doubt that was the intention, but it's not hard to see how this catch-all list might lead readers who aren't lawyers (a category that includes police officers) to take a very broad view of what counts, for reporting and recording purposes, as 'hate'.

In 2024 the government of the Australian state of Victoria conducted a public consultation on a proposed new 'anti-vilification' law; one of its proposals was to introduce a new offence of 'incit[ing] hatred, serious contempt, revulsion or severe ridicule against another person or group based on their protected attribute'.[27] One question this wording immediately raises is what the adjectives *serious* and *severe* mean. If what's defined as an offence is inciting 'serious' contempt rather than just contempt, that logically implies the existence of a less serious kind of contempt which will not be an offence. But the legislation doesn't spell out where the line is between the two. On what basis will the police or the courts decide whether contempt is 'serious'?

There's an argument that this is not really a particular problem with anti-hate laws. Many other kinds of legislation contain vague or general terms whose precise meaning is not spelled out. Laws against careless driving, for instance, don't specify exactly how careless driving has to be to get a driver arrested: it's assumed that there's a broad consensus which people can use to make reasonable judgments in particular circumstances. But arguably that's exactly where the problem with current anti-hate legislation lies – in the lack of any broad consensus on what kinds of speech are hateful enough to be dealt with by the law. The cases discussed in this chapter illustrate not only how little agreement there is, but also how strongly people's judgments of the gravity of the offence in particular cases are linked to their political allegiances: they are liable to deem offences more serious if the political view being expressed is one they condemn, and less serious if it is one they support.[28] If Victoria's proposal becomes law, it seems inevitable that there will be disputes about whether what an accused person expressed should count as 'serious contempt', and it's not clear how such disputes can be resolved without political bias.

In fact, though, the offence Victoria proposes to create isn't *expressing* serious contempt but *inciting* it, and that also raises questions. In ordinary language 'inciting' something means persuading or encouraging another person to do that thing; in legal contexts it usually means persuading or encouraging them to commit a criminal act (as with the Facebook post mentioned in Chapter 3 which exhorted rioters to 'blow up the Mosque with the adults inside'). But what does *incite* mean when the following word denotes not an action but a feeling (e.g., hate, contempt, revulsion)? Can feelings be incited? And if they can, will a speaker's own expression of contempt or revulsion automatically be taken as inciting others to feel contempt or revulsion, or are those two separate issues?

In Scotland's Hate Crime and Public Order Act, which came into force in 2024, the terminology used is not 'inciting' but 'stirring up' hatred, though this appears to mean much the same thing – engaging in 'conduct which encourages others to hate a particular group of people'. This part of the Act was controversial: critics complained that it was drawn so broadly (covering the use or sharing of 'threatening, abusive or insulting words, behaviour, material, images or sounds') that the police would be unable to cope with the volume of reported cases, and there were worries that the inclusion of 'insulting' would encourage trivial and/or vexatious complaints. But it was also criticized for a completely different reason. As the legal scholar Laura Higson-Bliss pointed out, stirring up racial hatred was already against the law: it has been an offence in Scotland since 1986, but only a handful of cases have been successfully prosecuted.[29] Many attempts have failed because in practice it's so difficult to prove (as prosecutors were required to do under the old law and will also have to do under the new one) that a defendant's words were either 'intended' to stir up hatred or 'likely' to stir up hatred. Rather than debate the exact wording of anti-hate legislation, Higson-Bliss thinks we should ask whether the criminal law is an effective tool for dealing with the problem. What's really needed, she suggests, is a shift in social attitudes and behavioural norms which is more likely to be achieved through 'public debate and better education'. But in that case, we might ask, why are legislators around the world currently so keen to introduce anti-hate laws or strengthen their existing ones?

There's a clue, perhaps, in the documents governments produce when they're either consulting the public about a proposed new law or informing them about a law that's about to come into force. The Scottish government published numerous documents of this kind about the Hate Crimes and Public Order Act, and it's striking how much emphasis they give to the symbolic function of the legislation. When they explain why they're proposing to extend the earlier 'stirring up racial hatred' provision to hatred based on other characteristics (age, disability, religion, sexuality and transgender identity), these texts say that the government wants to 'send a clear message' that society condemns prejudice against those groups, and that hateful behaviour towards them 'will not be tolerated'. But while all laws in all societies 'send a message' about what will not be tolerated, that message will only carry weight if the law is, and is seen to be, capable of bringing those who break it to justice. If it doesn't also fulfil that practical function its symbolic value is undermined. The message will appear to be performative, not in the technical sense explained in Chapter 2, but in the everyday pejorative sense of being no more than a performance or show of concern which does not, in reality, change anything.

I'm not suggesting that the people who make these laws are not sincerely committed to eradicating hate. Legislators, perhaps unsurprisingly, do tend to believe that legislation is an effective way to curb behaviour society disapproves of. So do many political activists (hence the fact that so many campaigns have changing the law as their main objective). But some would say that belief is naïve. As critical legal scholars have argued for decades, changing what the law says won't necessarily change either what it accomplishes or who benefits from it in practice.

The stories I've told in this chapter raise questions about the idea that extending the concept of hate speech and adopting definitions that reflect victims' perceptions will advance the cause of social justice by making powerful people accountable for the effects their words have on others. Though from a progressive point of view there are good reasons why that idea took root (I am not going to deny that institutional bias exists and is a frequent cause of injustice), its adoption in practice has not had the desired effect. In many of the cases I've mentioned the complainants were not victims of hate speech (they didn't themselves belong to the group they claimed another person's words had harmed), and those they accused of hate speech were not powerful. Some were grassroots protestors whose messages offended someone with more power; others, like the student who said veganism was wrong or the woman who photographed a sticker, were people whose words or actions were of so little consequence that pursuing complaints against them was at best a waste of time and at worst an abuse of authority. Many of the individuals who were punished most severely were targets of a modern form of vigilantism: draconian action was taken against them, often in haste and without investigation, to placate an online mob – though only if they were dispensable, like Gillian Philip. Mysteriously, the publisher of the hugely profitable Harry Potter books has not felt the same need to placate campaigners who want to cancel J. K. Rowling.

I find it hard to see anything progressive about any of this. But I also have problems with some of the arguments which are commonly made against it – for instance, those that criticize 'snowflakes' for getting upset about 'hurty words'. As I've already said more than once, whether and how language causes harm is a central preoccupation for both proponents and critics of contemporary dogwhistle politics. But tribal divisions and animosities have made this a highly polarized debate: there's a tendency for both sides to take extreme positions, either insisting that words are 'literal violence' or else maintaining that they are totally inconsequential. In the next chapter I'll explore these arguments in more detail.

5

'Literal Violence'? Dogwhistle Politics and the Language of Harm

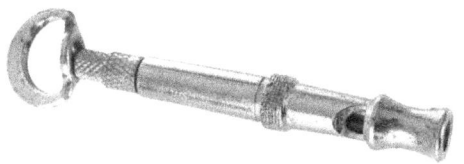

One summer afternoon in 1968, a nine-year-old girl walking home from school took her usual shortcut through a narrow alleyway that connected the main road to the housing estate where she lived. Halfway down the alley she was intercepted: a boy she recognized from school but had never spoken to (he was in the year above her) stepped out of the shadows and grabbed her. He pushed her against the wall and punched her three times, hard, in the face. Then he turned around and walked back towards the main road. He was silent throughout; when the girl got home, her nose bleeding and her face beginning to bruise, she could not give her horrified mother any explanation for what had happened.

As a teenager a few years later the girl was bullied for several months by a group of her classmates. They didn't use, or threaten, physical violence; instead they shunned her, refusing to speak to her directly, while taking every opportunity to tell each other in her presence what a horrible and disgusting person she was. Eventually they stopped, but the experience stayed with her. She found it far more painful to recall than the incident in the alleyway, which had been shocking, but also random and senseless. What the bullies did went deeper. For years, without willing it, she would sometimes hear their voices in her head.

I've told this story – my own story, but many people have had similar experiences – to underline the point that words can hurt and words can harm. The advice generations of children have been given ('Ignore them. Remember, sticks and stones can break my bones but words can never hurt me') is well-intentioned but unrealistic. I'm not the only person who has found verbal assaults more painful than being punched. In the early 1980s I belonged to a support group that helped to run a refuge for women escaping domestic abuse, and those women quite often said the same. Their abusers hadn't just assaulted them, often they'd made a point of explaining why. Sometimes it was a punishment for something the woman had done, or failed to do; sometimes it was because of something she supposedly was – a whore, or a stupid bitch, or so useless that anyone who had to live with her would want to punch her. Many of these women had been told repeatedly that they were worthless, and many of them had come to believe it. The damage that does is real, and often harder to fix than broken bones.

The belief that words can cause harm isn't new: it's reflected in everyday expressions (e.g., 'her words cut me to the quick') that have been around for centuries. But current views on this subject are highly polarized, and extreme claims are made on both sides. As I noted at the end of the last chapter, critics of 'wokeness' sometimes disparage people who complain about 'hurty words' as 'snowflakes', as if objecting to slurs and threats put them on a par with the apocryphal Victorian ladies who would faint if anyone mentioned the legs of a piano. But the people they're criticizing are also prone to hyperbole, accusing others of hate speech or 'literal violence' in circumstances where that seems disproportionate if not downright irrational. In this chapter I'll explore some of these conflicting claims, and try to assess the evidence for and against them.

Dangerous words: language as an incitement to violence

One way in which it is widely agreed that words can cause harm is by encouraging or persuading those who hear them to engage in acts of physical violence. Many societies place legal restrictions on speech that incites violence, and in clear cases of incitement (e.g., the Facebook post I mentioned in Chapter 3, 'blow up the Mosque with the adults inside'), which involve direct and linguistically transparent messages exhorting others to commit a specific act of violence, this is relatively uncontroversial. Though the producers of such messages can be convicted of incitement whether or not their words were actually acted on,[1] part of the rationale for making verbal incitement a criminal offence is the presumption that words are capable of provoking actions directly. But many discussions of hate speech assert that language leads to violence in a more indirect way, by creating, over time, a climate in which hostility to certain groups is so strong as to make people feel justified in using violence against them.

This way of thinking about the harmful effects of language developed in response to the modern phenomenon of genocide, the actual or attempted extermination of an entire group of people, for which the prototype was, and still is, the Holocaust. The role played by language in the genocide of the Jews was addressed at the Nuremberg Trials which followed the defeat of the Nazis in 1945. Among the war criminals who were tried and ultimately executed was Julius Streicher, the publisher of *Der Stürmer*, a newspaper that had been a key vehicle for disseminating antisemitic propaganda. Though Streicher had never ordered or directly participated in the killing of Jews, the court decided that his activities as a propagandist made him an accessory: his speeches and published writing were said to have inculcated in the German people the attitudes and feelings that made 'persecution in the first instance, and finally, the program of mass murder which he openly advocated, a psychological possibility'.[2]

This idea of 'psychological possibility' occupies an important place in accounts of the relationship between language and violence. Most people, the argument goes, will not condone, still less participate in, mass killing unless they have first been conditioned not to think of the victims as human beings like themselves. It is the othering and dehumanization of the target group, accomplished primarily through propaganda (language and images), that makes killing them seem possible and acceptable. This point has often been made in connection with the wartime use of derogatory and dehumanizing labels (like *Hun* or *Gook*) for members of the enemy group: though killing is understood to be permissible in war, dehumanizing the enemy is said to make it easier. In cases like Nazi Germany, where the victims lived alongside their persecutors as fellow-citizens, neighbours and sometimes friends, the dehumanizing process may require more time and effort. Its effect depends on repetition – constantly reiterating the same messages in the same words until eventually they become normalized and taken for granted.

This argument featured prominently in analyses of the genocide that took place in Rwanda in 1994, when in the space of about three months an estimated 800,000+ people, mainly from the Tutsi minority, were killed by members of the Hutu majority. Many accounts of these events emphasized the contribution made over a long period of time by hate speech in the media, and particularly by two government-aligned radio stations whose output relentlessly demonized and dehumanized Tutsis, referring to them as *inyenzi* ('cockroach') and *inzoka* ('snake'). The Nazis had used the same rhetorical strategy of representing their targets as verminous or dangerous animals. It seemed likely, therefore, that the International Criminal Tribunal for Rwanda (ICTR), relying on the precedent established at Nuremberg, would convict the broadcasters who spread that message of inciting genocide. But while the initial trial did find a number of them guilty, the verdicts were overturned on appeal – in part because judges took the view that the evidence for a causal link between the broadcasts and the killings was 'at the very least, tenuous'.

This appeal judgment was criticized for being legally incoherent. International courts are supposed to adhere to the principle mentioned earlier, whereby proving incitement does not require evidence that the messages which constituted the incitement led directly to acts of violence. Many experts were worried about the precedent the ICTR judgment set, because if evidence of direct causation were required almost all incitement cases would fail. As the human rights lawyer and activist Susan Benesch explains, direct causation is virtually impossible to prove in court because 'the effect of speech on large groups of people is hard to measure, poorly understood, and is only one of a constellation of forces that affect why people act as they do'.[3]

This is an important point, not only in relation to criminal proceedings but in general, and it is too often underplayed or glossed over in contemporary debates about harmful speech – especially on the progressive left, where theories that accord language a special power to direct our thoughts and our behaviour have been very influential. What happened in Rwanda has often been cited as compelling evidence for the power of language: online searching throws up countless articles with headings like 'How hate speech triggered genocide' and 'When words kill'. But there are reasons to think that narrative may have overstated the role of hate speech. Many people who took part in the killings had had no exposure to broadcast propaganda (some poorer Rwandans had no access to a radio, and there were numerous settlements where there was no radio reception). Rather they were recruited via networks of male kinsfolk and were induced to participate by a combination of family loyalties and fear of the consequences of not participating (though most genocide victims were Tutsis, some were Hutus who had declined to join in the violence).[4]

But to say that hate speech was 'only one of a constellation of forces' that led to genocide in Rwanda is not to say that it played no role at all. Even if it isn't the root cause of violent conflict, language may help to fan the flames, or as the social psychologists Jeff Greenberg and Tom Pyzsczynski once put it, 'spread a social disease'.[5]

Troublesome words: disputes about slurs

The 'social disease' Greenberg and Pyzsczynski were referring to was racism: the phrase appeared in the title of an article about a racial slur, the N-word (I'll say more about their study later on). Slurs are prototype examples of hate speech, expressing prejudice and contempt in a way that has no plausible deniability, and it is generally accepted among people who study them that their use has harmful effects on the people they target.[6] To address or refer to an individual with a slur term is more than just insulting: it is a way of putting them in their socially allotted place as an inferior and an object of contempt, and the effect may be to shame and humiliate them, to cause fear and emotional distress, and to reduce them to silence (which arguably deprives them of the free speech rights that the slur-user claims for him or herself). The use of slurs can also license discriminatory treatment of the group as a whole by recycling the stereotypes which have historically justified that treatment. In recent years this understanding of the harm caused by slurs has led to a situation where a number of the most offensive terms, such as the N-word, are not just disapproved of but – unless you actively want to communicate that you're a bigot – taboo, literally unspeakable. Not only must their actual use be avoided, if you need to refer to them in the way I've just referred to the N-word you must substitute some other form, like 'the N-word', for the full, unexpurgated slur.

Yet even slur terms can mean more than one thing. They can be used, for instance, as markers of solidarity, intimacy and trust among members of the target group (even the N-word can serve this purpose), and some have been 'reclaimed' as positive identity labels (e.g., *queer*, which in my own youth was unequivocally a homophobic slur). They are not, in short, an exception to the rule that meaning depends on context, and disputes can therefore arise about how the utterance of a slur should be interpreted.

One dispute of this kind arose in 2020, when a professor of business communication at the University of Southern California was suspended by the Dean of the business school after a group of students in his class complained that he had repeatedly used a Chinese filler phrase that sounded like the English N-word.[7] There was no dispute that the professor had used the phrase in question ('nei ge'): he was teaching about the use of filled pauses (equivalent to English 'um' and 'er') and giving examples in a range of languages. What was disputed was whether it was reasonable either for the students to interpret his use of the phrase as racist or for the institution to discipline him on that basis. The Dean clearly thought it was: in an email to the class he wrote that 'it is simply unacceptable for faculty to use words in class that can marginalize, hurt and harm the psychological safety of our students'. However, his action prompted other students to sign a petition calling for the professor to be reinstated. 'For him to be censored simply because a Chinese word sounds like an English pejorative term is a mistake', it said: '[it] dismisses the fact that Chinese is a real language and has its own pronunciations that have no relation to English'.

Like the 'almond eyes' controversy discussed in Chapter 4, this dispute raised the question of whose understanding of language should be accorded more authority, and whose feelings about it should be given more weight, in a situation where two groups (in this case, black students and Chinese-speaking students) disagreed. But other people who read about the case had a more basic question. If the students knew, as in the context of the class they surely must have known, that the professor wasn't actually saying the N-word, he was saying the Mandarin equivalent of 'um', how could they have perceived that as a threat? Why did they apparently see no difference between intentionally using a racial slur and demonstrating the use of a phrase in a foreign language?

Similar questions may be asked about cases where the offending expression isn't in a foreign language. Sometimes complaining about the utterance of a certain word means making no distinction between 'use' and 'mention' – the terms used to capture the difference between saying, for instance, 'geography was my worst subject at school' and saying 'I've always found "geography" hard to spell'. In the latter case you are not using the word *geography* but mentioning it; in writing you'd indicate that by putting it in quotation marks (or italics, if you're a linguist – we mention words a lot). Similarly, if someone in a class about taboo words uttered a slur term to illustrate or clarify what they were talking about they would be mentioning the slur term, not using it. In other cases the offending term might appear in an actual quotation, perhaps from a historical text pre-dating the current taboo, or from a literary work where the author put a slur term in the mouth of a character to show that the character was a bigot. Over the years there have been regular calls for schools and colleges to stop teaching novels like Mark Twain's *Huckleberry Finn* and John Steinbeck's *Of Mice And Men* because of their characters' prolific use of the N-word, though both authors are clearly opposed to racism, which they dramatize in order to criticize. Or the term that prompts complaint might be being used metaphorically, in reference to someone or something entirely different. One academic I know had a student who objected strenuously to the use of the term 'pink-collar ghetto' in writing by economists about gender segregation in the labour market.

This isn't only an issue in educational contexts. Towards the end of the 2010s a consensus emerged that one of the most popular Christmas songs of the last half-century, 'Fairytale of New York' (originally released in 1988 by the Pogues with Kirsty MacColl), could no longer be played by mainstream radio or TV stations. The song is a duet between a woman and a man (in the original recording, MacColl and the Pogues' Shane MacGowan) playing the roles of two mid-twentieth-century Irish immigrants to New York – people who arrived with high hopes when they were young, but have since fallen on hard times. During the song they abuse each other in a rapid-fire exchange that includes the words 'you scumbag/you maggot/you cheap lousy faggot'. All these words (apart from *you*) are offensive, but the one that made the song unplayable was the homophobic slur *faggot*. MacGowan, who wrote the lyric, pointed out that it's a story about people of a certain type in a particular time and place, and said he had chosen words he thought those people would have used: he was not endorsing their sentiments or their language. This explanation, however, did little to shift the twenty-first-century conviction that some words cannot be tolerated in any context.

In fact, the view I've just called a 'twenty-first-century conviction' has a much longer history in relation to certain slur terms. In 2002 the African American legal scholar Randall Kennedy published a book called *N----: The Strange Career of a Troublesome Word*, in which he surveyed the history of both legal cases and other public controversies about the use of the N-word in the US.[8] Re-reading it today is a reminder that concern about the harmful effects of words, and especially of this particular word, is nothing new – but it's also a reminder of what has changed in the space of twenty years. Whereas I've just rendered Kennedy's title in expurgated form, the word that actually appears on the cover of his book, as well as innumerable times in the text, is spelled out in full. That choice was controversial in 2002 (indeed, the book shows it would also have been controversial in 1952 or 1922), but today we might wonder if any mainstream publisher would allow an author to make it.

Kennedy's views about the N-word were also somewhat controversial, and they are certainly at odds with today's progressive orthodoxy. One legal debate he considers concerns what is known as the 'mere words' doctrine, according to which words on their own, however derogatory and inflammatory, cannot be the basis for a defence of provocation (the argument that someone who committed a crime was provoked by their victim and should therefore be convicted of a less serious offence, e.g., manslaughter rather than murder). Most (though not all) US states adhere to this doctrine, but it has long been argued that an exception should be made for the N-word on the grounds that it is not a 'mere word', it is 'a form of violence by speech', and thus comparable to the kind of physical violence which has always been recognized as a legitimate basis for provocation claims. Kennedy ultimately comes down in favour of allowing juries to consider whether a defendant's actions were provoked by the victim's language, and if so whether that should be treated as a mitigating factor. But he is clearly ambivalent, saying that for him 'the issue is agonizingly close, with strong arguments on both sides'.[9] And he has no time at all for claims that language has harmed or provoked if there is no clear evidence that it was deliberately used for that purpose.

One case he discusses centred, like the more recent dispute involving the USC professor, on a word that sounded like, but was not, the N-word. In 1999 the white director of a municipal agency in Washington, DC was forced to resign after using the word *niggardly* while talking to his staff about the budget cuts the agency faced. The interaction was not public, but it was made public by staff members who found the use of *niggardly* offensive. Their complaint was then amplified by media commentators who, like them, were African American. But some of the director's most vocal defenders were also African American. Opinion among black commentators was divided: while some asked why, if the director was not a racist, he had not chosen some other word (e.g., *miserly*), others expressed impatience with, as one put it, 'people whose antennae are always up, seeking out an affront where none exists so they can respond out of all proportion'. Kennedy is clearly in the second camp, calling the ousting of the director a 'wrong-headed protest' that 'will forever . . . serve as a benchmark of hypersensitivity'.[10]

By contrast, some linguists and philosophers have argued that this kind of response is not unreasonable or disproportionate: it's related to a property of slurs known technically as 'hyperprojectivity', meaning they have the same or almost the same negative effect on members of the target group when merely mentioned as when directly used. (One experimental study showed that the effect is slightly weaker if the slur is used in an indirect quotation, but the same is not true for direct quotations, and even the weaker effect is still significant.[11]) For these scholars it is incumbent on speakers who don't belong to the target group to recognize that slurs have this property, and to avoid saying or writing anything that will trigger the negative effect. From that perspective, speakers like the white director and the USC professor may not be guilty of deliberate racism, but they are guilty of a form of culpable negligence.[12]

But in the *niggardly* case there were black commentators who evidently did make the distinction this argument implies people targeted by racial slurs do not (or perhaps even cannot) make. The point that members of the same minority group may respond differently to words or utterances is one Kennedy emphasizes throughout the book, along with the point that the N-word has a range of functions and meanings, not all of which are necessarily malign. For him a blanket prohibition on any word, even one with as much oppressive historical baggage as the N-word, risks turning the word into a fetish and so giving it more power than it deserves.

It's perhaps telling that critics of the blanket prohibition approach use words like 'taboo' and 'fetish', which originally referred to beliefs and practices observed by European colonialists in traditional non-western cultures (*taboo* originates in the South Pacific, and means a prohibition which is observed to protect people from harm, while *fetish* is derived from the French word denoting an object believed to have magical powers). If uttering a certain sequence of sounds can produce the same harmful effect regardless of what the utterance means in context or even what language it belongs to, that might well remind us of 'word magic', an umbrella term for practices based on the belief that some linguistic formulas have an inherent power which can either be harnessed (e.g., by using them in spells, incantations or religious rituals) or neutralized (by prohibiting their utterance), but which humans are not the source of and whose effects they cannot control.

But you don't have to believe in magic to think that some words might have a particular kind of power, deriving not from supernatural forces but from historical and social ones. Some research evidence suggests that slurs might be a case in point. Randall Kennedy cites an example – the study I've already mentioned by Greenberg and Pyzsczynski, which was published in 1985, and whose subtitle was 'how to spread a social disease'. In the experiment these researchers conducted, white subjects were asked to score the participants in a series of debates where one contestant was black and the other was white. After each debate, confederates (students who had been recruited to carry out the researchers' instructions while pretending to be experimental subjects) engaged in an interaction others could overhear, in which they either made no comment or else commented negatively on the black debater. In some cases the negative comment was not racially specific, while in others it contained the N-word. The question was what effect overhearing these comments would have on white subjects' assessments of the debate. The researchers found that subjects who overheard the N-word showed a strong tendency to give black debaters lower scores. They pointed out that if this effect held across a wider range of contexts there would be many situations in which the stakes were far higher – for instance, parole board or jury deliberations – where the casual use of a slur by one individual might influence the decision of the whole group, to the detriment of the person whose case was being considered.

Experiments have also been carried out to investigate whether homophobic slurs trigger bias against, and discriminatory behaviour towards, gay men. One study presented heterosexual subjects with wordlists that included either a non-derogatory category label (such as *gay*) or a homophobic slur (the research was done in Italy, so the item chosen was the Italian term *frocio*, which is comparable to *faggot* in English), and asked them some questions about the words. Then they were presented with a hypothetical scenario in which the council had been given some money to support preventive healthcare, and two groups had applied for funding. One group was working on preventing infertility (stereotypically a problem affecting heterosexuals), while the other was seeking support for their work on preventing HIV-AIDS (stereotypically, at least in Europe, a problem affecting gay men). Subjects were asked how much money they thought should be allocated to each group of applicants. Those who had been presented with the slur term showed a greater tendency to favour the infertility programme over the HIV-AIDS programme.[13] In a subsequent study, a team that included some of the same researchers found that subjects who'd been subliminally primed with homophobic slurs (shown a word like *faggot* for a few milliseconds while completing an unrelated visual task on screen) chose to sit further away from an interviewer they believed to be a gay man than subjects who had been primed in the same way with either a category label (e.g., *gay*) or a more generic insult (e.g., *asshole*).[14] The subjects were students who do not seem to have been overtly homophobic: they reported having, on average, three or four gay friends. But exposure to homophobic slur terms still had a significant effect on their behaviour.

As usual with experiments there are some caveats we should bear in mind. People's responses to slur terms under less controlled conditions, or in contexts like the ones which have prompted accusations of overreacting (e.g., where the word is not actually a slur, or where the slur is being mentioned rather than used, or where its use is clearly meant to be ironic), might differ from their responses in the experimental situation (where in all cases the stimulus was an actual slur, presented either without context or in a context where it was clearly intended to be negative). And of course, these studies were not designed to investigate whether exposure to racist or homophobic slurs causes psychological harm to black or gay people, which is a different question from whether slurs harm those people by triggering other people's prejudice against them.

If we listen to the personal testimony of group members then there's no doubt slurs have negative psychological effects. But if we're looking for evidence to support the argument that they are and should be treated as a special case, the question is whether these particular terms cause more serious harm than any other form of speech which derogates a group of people. Is it more harmful to a gay man to hear someone say 'faggots are disgusting' than to hear them say 'gay men are disgusting'? A lot of theoretical work on slurs suggests the answer to that question should be yes, but I'm not sure we have strong evidence to back that up. Some research has investigated the physiological effects of being insulted or verbally abused. The authors of one study done in the Netherlands, which used EEG and skin conductance readings to gauge the effects of insults like 'Paula is horrible' or 'Linda is an idiot', describe the effect as comparable to being hit. 'Insults', they say, are 'lexical "minislaps in the face"'.[15] The same techniques might shed light on whether slurs produce a stronger effect than either insults like 'horrible' or identity labels like 'gay men', but conducting such a study would raise the ethical objection that if it turned out the effect was much stronger, the subjects would have suffered an unacceptable degree of harm.

The conclusions I draw from this discussion are mixed. On one hand I think there's a pretty compelling argument for not using slurs, or even mentioning them, if you don't have to. On the other, I share Randall Kennedy's view that banning words outright is a crude and potentially counterproductive strategy which gives too little consideration to the fact that their meanings and functions are variable and context dependent. It also disregards the possibility that prohibiting the use of a word to protect one minority might infringe the rights of another – for instance, the right of Mandarin speakers at USC to have their language treated with respect. For me these are conflicts that need to be discussed and negotiated rather than problems that can be solved by just decreeing a word to be off limits and punishing anyone who utters it for any reason (though that's not to say I think it's necessarily a bad thing if speakers feel social pressure to avoid certain words).

Commonplace words: microaggressions

Not all academics who write about slurs regard them as a special case. In their book *The Politics of Language*, for instance, the linguist David Beaver and the philosopher Jason Stanley argue that any way of speaking or writing that devalues a group will have harmful effects: this applies as much to coded expressions of prejudice like dogwhistles as to overt and undisguised ones like slurs. In his writing on dogwhistles as propaganda, Stanley sometimes seems to be suggesting (and as we'll see, he is not alone) that coded messages are if anything even more harmful than transparent ones: they transfer the qualities and effects of slurs onto utterances that appear to be innocuous, making the intent to harm deniable and thus harder to hold the speaker to account for.

It's this more radical view of language and harm that's most likely to prompt conflict between 'woke' activists and their critics. There are many people, including people of moderate or even somewhat conservative political views, who don't think it's unreasonable for the state to criminalize incitements to violence, or for institutions like universities and workplaces to treat the (deliberate) use of slurs as a disciplinary matter. These are readily seen as clear violations both of other people's rights and of the norms of civil discourse. But the same people may have serious reservations about extending that approach to cases where it's not clear either that the speaker intended to harm anyone or that any harm was actually caused.

One area where these reservations may come to the fore is in disputes about alleged 'microaggressions', classically defined as 'brief and commonplace daily verbal, behavioral and environmental indignities, whether intentional or unintentional, that communicate hostile, derogatory or negative ... slights and insults to the target person or group'.[16] Verbal microaggressions share some features with dogwhistles: they are seemingly innocuous remarks from which members of the target group can infer prejudice or disrespect, while non-members typically do not make that inference. Microaggressions differ from dogwhistles, however, in that they are more likely to communicate prejudice unintentionally. The meaning that leads their recipients to find them offensive may be hidden not only from other people who hear the message, but also from the person who actually sent it.

One much-discussed example of this type of verbal microaggression is when a member of a society's majority group (e.g., a white American in the US) asks someone who is identifiable as a member of a minority ethnic group (e.g., a Latino co-worker) where they 'come from'. The speaker may think she's just being friendly, but what she's communicating to her co-worker is the racist assumption that a brown-skinned person with a Spanish name must be an immigrant or a foreigner rather than a fellow-citizen. Of course, that might not be her intention. Maybe she'd put the same question to anyone she hadn't met before, and she wouldn't be at all surprised if the answer were 'Cleveland' rather than 'Colombia'. But it's been argued that the inherent ambiguity of microaggressions – the fact that you can't be sure if you're being addressed in a certain way because of your race/ethnicity (or gender or sexuality) – makes them particularly harmful, because the uncertainty is a source of additional stress. The 'micro'-ness of microaggressions is also said to be a problem. Negative reactions to small insults are easily dismissed as overreactions, but that overlooks the point that their harmful effect is cumulative. It's not any single occurrence of 'where are you from?', or 'hey, your English is really good!' that does the damage, it's being constantly reminded of the way others perceive you by hearing the same thing over and over.

Is it reasonable to expect people like the white speaker in my example to avoid verbal microaggressions in the same way they would (in most cases) avoid overtly bigoted language? Up to a point, I'd say yes. We all understand, as part of our everyday 'communicative competence', that some people have linguistic sensitivities which we should be willing to accommodate if we want to maintain cordial relations with them. That's why, for instance, we might try to avoid profanity when talking to a colleague we know is very religious: making a certain amount of conscious effort not to offend our interlocutors is, in most situations, our standard operating procedure. But radical identity politics has encouraged an approach to microaggressions which goes beyond calls to show respect and consideration by thinking about what might offend people whose beliefs are different from yours. Some definitions of what's offensive or disrespectful are so expansive that disputes and conflicts about them have become a regular occurrence.

One contentious issue is illustrated by the reaction of a Latino student soccer player to the use of the word *futbol* (Spanish for football/soccer) by an Anglo teammate. He reported this on a website which had been set up to collect examples of microaggressions, saying he had told his teammate to 'get my language out of your mouth'.[17] It's not clear if there was something objectionable about the utterance beyond the use of a Spanish word (e.g., if the Anglo player used a mocking tone or a parodic Spanish accent), but if there wasn't – if the point was simply that majority group members are disrespecting minorities by 'appropriating' their culture (speaking their language, wearing their clothes and hairstyles, cooking their foods, etc.) – then to many people it isn't obvious why that should be considered disrespectful. Cultures, after all, have always influenced and borrowed from one another: *futbol*, the Spanish version of the English word for a game invented in England, is an obvious example.

An even more contentious issue is defining the expression of certain political views as a microaggression. In 2014 the University of California system produced some materials for use in faculty training courses which included, as examples of microaggressions, the statements 'America is a melting pot' and 'I believe the most qualified person should get the job'. Though they are certainly contested, these views are hardly extreme: there are liberals as well as conservatives who would defend them. But by calling them microaggressions the university seemed to be suggesting that they should not be debated in UC classrooms.

There are also cases where *not* expressing a certain view may be regarded as a microaggression. This issue has arisen in some institutions whose policies call for staff to state their preferred pronouns by, say, wearing a badge that displays them or including them in an email signature. Because one function of this practice is to show support for trans and nonbinary people, not engaging in it may be seen as a coded expression of hostility to those groups. However, pronoun-sharing also has the function of declaring a speaker or writer's own gender identity, and people who don't want to do that – either because they consider it private information or because they don't subscribe to the belief system that includes the concept of gender identity – have objected to policies mandating it as 'compelled speech', not unlike requiring employees to end their emails with 'Praise the Lord' or 'God save the King'.[18]

Like incitements and slurs, microaggressions are sometimes described as violence, and that causes controversy in its own right. While of course words can be used figuratively as well as literally, there are limits on what most people consider to be a legitimate use of the word *violence* to describe acts or experiences which do not involve the use or the threat of physical force. Many might have some sympathy for the description I quoted earlier of the N-word as 'a form of violence through speech', but fewer would sympathize with the Oxford student who used the word *violence* to describe having to pass a statue of the imperialist Cecil Rhodes on his way to class.[19] Between those two extremes, however, there are cases in which it could be argued – and has been, by some researchers – that the comparison of speech with violence is not just overblown rhetoric.

In an opinion piece she wrote for the *New York Times* in 2017, the psychologist Lisa Feldman Barrett explicitly considered the question 'When is speech violence?' Her answer was, in essence, when it causes a kind and degree of stress that is known to have long-term ill-effects on mental and/or physical health.[20] There is certainly evidence that speech on its own can cause a detectable increase in stress, such as the study I cited earlier which found the effect of exposure to insults like '[you're] horrible/an idiot' was comparable to the effect of being slapped. But whereas that effect was short-lived, causing only the kind of momentary stress Barrett argues humans are equipped to withstand, she thinks there are reasons to be concerned about the effects of more sustained verbal abuse. Research using neuroimaging techniques to study the brains of adults with a childhood history of being regularly verbally abused (but not otherwise mistreated) by either their parents or their peers has found abnormalities in certain areas of their brains; these subjects' medical histories also show an 'elevated vulnerability to psychiatric disorders' such as depression, substance abuse and excessive anger. The same pattern is seen in adults with childhood histories of physical or sexual abuse.[21]

But assessing this kind of evidence is complicated. As the researchers themselves acknowledge, retrospective studies cannot show that any observed brain abnormalities were directly caused by childhood verbal abuse. It also seems likely that what the subjects in these studies experienced – being regularly abused over a period of time by people they were close to, cared about and depended on – is more damaging than being insulted or patronized by strangers and casual acquaintances. But in addition, it's been suggested that the effects of verbal abuse may be mediated by culture. There's some experimental evidence that people from groups with different cultural beliefs about insults (e.g., about how damaging they are and how strongly a person should react to them) have different physiological responses to being insulted.[22] That might raise a question I mentioned in passing in a previous chapter: is the kind of sensitivity on display in campus disputes about microaggressions the result of today's young people being socialized into a 'victim culture' from which they've learned to treat every minor slight or inconsiderate remark as a hostile attack that threatens their safety?

Victimhood culture and the language of harm

Complaints about 'victim culture' are typically made by right-wing pundits for whom the term is unambiguously derogatory. But in the same way some academic writers have tried to give a more considered, descriptive account of 'wokeness', the sociologists Bradley Campbell and Jason Manning have taken a similar approach to 'victim culture' – or as they prefer to call it, 'victimhood culture' – using a framework developed in earlier studies of 'moral cultures'.[23]

The academic literature on moral cultures distinguishes two major types, one centred on *honour* and the other on *dignity*. In honour cultures (which were found in the majority of western societies until the modern era) a person's status in their community depends on maintaining a 'good name' or reputation: people are extremely sensitive to slights and insults, and their moral code requires such attacks to be avenged, often with violence (duelling and blood-feuding are both honour-culture practices). Not to defend your honour is considered shameful, weak and cowardly. There are still societies, and subcultures within societies (e.g., criminal gangs), where these norms persist, but honour culture was the product of social conditions (such as tight-knit, kin-based communities and the absence of a strong state apparatus for resolving disputes and suppressing violence) which are no longer the norm in most places. Modern social conditions favour a moral culture based on dignity, the idea that every person has an intrinsic worth which cannot be destroyed by insults, and that people display their worth by exercising dignified restraint in the face of provocation from others. In dignity cultures interpersonal violence is not seen as an acceptable way of resolving conflicts: serious disputes should be put in the hands of the authorities, while minor ones should be settled by negotiation. Children are taught that 'words will never hurt me' (i.e., that they should maintain their dignity when insulted); they are sanctioned for physical fighting and encouraged to appeal to adults for help in resolving disputes fairly.

Victimhood culture as Campbell and Manning describe it is a third type of moral culture which has some features of each of its predecessors. It retains the emphasis placed by dignity cultures on looking to the authorities to resolve disputes, but rejects the view that there is virtue in ignoring or minimizing slights: on that point it is more like honour culture, treating even minor insults as serious threats. But one thing that differentiates victimhood culture from honour culture is the way those threats are talked about – not in the old language of honour and 'satisfaction' (what a gentleman demanded when he challenged someone to a duel), but in what Campbell and Manning call a 'language of harm', which emphasizes the aggrieved person or group's vulnerability, and demands intervention to protect them and make them safe.

The rise of victimhood culture is especially visible among students at elite universities, for whom the language of harm seems largely to have displaced other ways of talking about social (in)justice. If you're old enough to remember the student activism of the 1970s and 1980s this is a very striking change in both activists' rhetoric and their demands. For instance, when my generation of literature students campaigned for the syllabus to be less narrowly focused on the writing of Dead White Men, what we mostly attacked was the paternalistic idea that we weren't entitled to any say in what we studied. By contrast, a recent demand to diversify the reading list for a literature course at Yale asserted that students would be 'actively harmed' by studying a syllabus that contained no work by non-white, female or queer writers. As a student in the late 1970s protesting against violence against women I carried a placard that said 'Women Are Angry'. Nearly forty years later, black students protesting against racism on a campus where I once worked carried placards that said 'We Are Not OK'.

The politicized language of harm draws directly on the concepts and terminology of psychiatry and psychotherapy (e.g., *safe space, trauma, trigger*). That isn't new: it has been happening in radical leftist subcultures since at least the 1960s. But as we saw earlier in the book, in recent decades psychotherapy itself has adopted more expansive definitions of harm, and that is also evident in the thinking and rhetoric of today's progressive activists. The psychologist Nick Haslam, who has written extensively about this 'concept creep', believes it has both benefits and costs. It is no bad thing, he suggests, if we've become more compassionate in our attitudes to people suffering from mental distress, and more aware that common experiences like being bullied at school or work can have serious long-term repercussions. But he also thinks this increased sensitivity can manifest itself in ways which are dysfunctional rather than helpful. When terms like *abuse* and *violence* are applied almost indiscriminately to an ever-wider range of cases, there is a risk of 'pathologizing everyday experience and encouraging a sense of virtuous but impotent victimhood'.[24]

In institutions like universities the problem noted by Haslam may be exacerbated by some of the actions taken in response to concerns about psychological harm, such as requiring staff and students to undergo diversity or anti-bias training. Though this is a popular type of intervention (one student activists have often pressured administrators to put in place), research has found that in practice it does not deliver the expected benefits. In the words of the researchers Frank Dobbin and Alexandra Kalev, 'there is ample evidence that [it] does not change attitudes or behavior, or not by much and not for long'.[25] As these writers go on to explain, there is also a well-attested tendency for anti-bias training to 'backfire', reinforcing the stereotypes it is meant to combat and prompting resentment among majority group members who feel they are being personally attacked. Consequently it may intensify rather than reduce inter-group conflict, and make the minority group members who put their faith in it feel even more like 'impotent victims'.[26]

It should not be thought, however, that victimhood culture and the language of harm are confined to elite campuses, or more generally to the 'woke' left; the same trends are visible at the other end of the social and political spectrum. The cultural narrative crafted by right-wing populists in the early decades of the present century is very much a narrative of victimhood, but with the traditional roles reversed: in this story the victims are white, male and Christian, while their oppressors are racial minorities, women and Muslims. Some right-wing activists have even emulated the rhetorical extremism of their adversaries. Campbell and Manning report on a 2017 protest against a production of Shakespeare's *Julius Caesar* which portrayed Caesar as a Trump-like demagogue: angry Trump supporters stormed the stage shouting 'This is violence against the right!'

But the linguistic norms of progressive victimhood culture have not gone unquestioned on the left itself. As I noted at the beginning of this book, 'woke' activism has been criticized by a number of progressive writers for overstating the importance of language as both a cause of and a remedy for social injustice. That criticism will be examined in the final chapter of this book.

6

#LanguageMatters

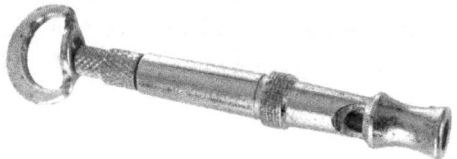

'Overstating the power of language', writes the sociologist Musa al-Gharbi, has led today's social justice movements to adopt a politics of 'symbolic gestures . . . [that] change virtually nothing about the allocation of wealth or power in society'. This preoccupation with words and symbols, he argues, tends to alienate, exclude and silence those who have the least wealth and power – not only because it fails to address their most pressing material concerns, but also because people who haven't been brought up in privileged households or educated at elite institutions are 'less likely to possess the cultural capital to say the "correct" things'.[1]

This is a common view among liberal and leftist critics of 'wokeness', and by the end of 2024 it seemed their criticisms had been prescient. Donald Trump's return to power was widely seen as signalling a popular backlash against all things 'woke'; in the weeks that followed his election victory there were numerous signs that the mood had changed. The 'woke' capitalism practised by many organizations turned out to be as shallow as sceptics had always thought: there was a steady stream of announcements from companies that they were rolling back or terminating their DEI programmes.[2] Mark Zuckerberg's Facebook followed Elon Musk's X in relaxing the platform's rules against hate speech and eliminating fact-checking to curb the spread of disinformation. It was even reported that several luminaries of the left had quietly removed their pronouns from their online profiles. 'Woke', the pundits said, was history. The people had spoken and the world had moved on.

But even if we bracket the point that the US is not the world, the fact that one side in a battle has wrested the advantage from the other does not mean the war is over. The conflicts over language I've been examining in this book are products and enactments of larger tendencies which shape the actions and the tactics of both sides. For as long as those tendencies remain in place, words and symbols will continue to be a battleground.

As if to demonstrate the point, in its first few weeks the Trump administration embarked on a concerted campaign to reclaim language for the right. The body of water formerly known as the Gulf of Mexico was unilaterally renamed 'the Gulf of America', and when the Associated Press declined to adopt the new name its representatives were denied access to White House press briefings.[3] Researchers who received funding from federal agencies were told that grants would be denied or rescinded if their proposals contained words the administration disapproved of; by the end of April 2025 the anti-censorship group PEN America had compiled a list of around 350 terms that had allegedly been banned, including *diversity, equity, identity, net zero, vaccines* and *women*.[4] I say 'allegedly', though, because it isn't clear how many of these items had been explicitly prohibited by the administration: in some cases their avoidance seems to have been an internal policy adopted pre-emptively by institutions in the hope that they would not lose funding (a classic example of the 'chilling effect', and a reminder that authoritarians of all stripes rely heavily on using fear to induce self-censorship). It was also reported that some much older documents containing forbidden words had been removed from government websites[5] – a move uncomfortably reminiscent of the continual rewriting of history which was Winston Smith's job in Orwell's *Nineteen Eighty-Four*.

Meanwhile, on the other side of the political fence, the preoccupation with words and symbols continued. On the day Trump took office and started issuing Executive Orders, the biggest talking-point among progressives on social media was quite literally a symbolic gesture – the one made by Elon Musk while speaking at a post-inauguration rally, which may or may not have been a Nazi salute.[6] Over the next few days I witnessed angry exchanges on X and Facebook in which questioning the fascist meaning of the gesture was equated with denying Musk's far-right sympathies – as if it were not possible to believe *both* that he has those sympathies *and* that his gesture probably wasn't a Nazi salute. In some progressive circles, being willing to say it was definitely a Nazi salute seemed to have become a kind of political loyalty test. What depressed me about this wasn't just the tribalism. The technique once memorably described by Steve Bannon as 'flooding the zone with shit' – using deliberately transgressive statements or gestures to grab attention, sow confusion and provoke outrage – has a history of being deployed by the right to divert the gaze of the media, and thus the public, from less spectacular but more politically consequential actions. If that was what Musk was trying to do, it worked. While opponents of the new administration were expressing outrage about his gesture, or arguing among themselves about what it meant, he and others got on with executing their plan to transform the political landscape (circumvent the checks and balances built into the US Constitution, decimate federally funded public services and neutralize the threat posed by 'enemy' institutions like universities, the press and the arts).

The issue here is balance: I'm not suggesting that language doesn't matter at all, or denying that it has real-world consequences. As we've seen, it can trigger biases that affect people's judgments without their knowledge, or produce reactions which are comparable to the effects of being hit. But you do not have to believe that language is trivial to wonder whether contemporary social justice movements overstate its political importance, and spend too much time and energy on forms of activism which are, as Musa al-Gharbi and others have argued, ineffective or counterproductive. That's what I'll be exploring in this final chapter. Is the attention given to language in social justice politics excessive? Is this an elitist preoccupation that excludes and alienates the very people 'woke' activists claim to speak for? Do 'symbolic gestures' accomplish anything worthwhile, or do they just cause resentment and increase polarization?

'Stop saying that!': the paranoid style in 'woke' language politics

'Do you remember', someone asked me recently, 'all those memes that went STOP SAYING [WORD]! NORMALIZE SAYING [DIFFERENT WORD]!' I did remember: when I first joined Twitter in the mid-2010s, the kind of message she meant was ubiquitous. It even had its own hashtag, #LanguageMatters, which I quickly learned to recognize as a sign that the tweet containing it would be doing one of two things: either condemning the language used by a political opponent or, more often, explaining to the tweeter's own tribe why some word or phrase they'd assumed was OK really wasn't OK at all.

Today the hashtag is less popular, but the kind of advice it accompanied is still alive and well. A random example that turned up in my Facebook feed just before I started writing this chapter was a four-year-old *Harvard Business Review* piece headed 'Why You Need to Stop Using These Words and Phrases'.[7] Its subject was ableist language, and its central point was that we should stop using words like *dumb*, *crazy*, *lame* and *stupid* as generic terms of disparagement, because that harms people with physical or cognitive disabilities. The author concedes that this is probably unintended: 'people use ableist language every day', she says, 'without realizing the harm they do'. But according to a series of experts she goes on to quote, using words like *dumb* and *lame* as criticisms stigmatizes people who are unable to speak or walk easily. In this case the proposed solution isn't to normalize non-ableist alternatives to the offending words: the view of the experts quoted seems to be that we shouldn't be using disparaging terms at all. One suggests that instead of calling Donald Trump a 'psycho' or a 'weirdo', we should concentrate on describing what it is about his policies we disagree with.

Like many examples of its genre, this advice combines a high level of moral outrage with a low level of practical utility, because it shows little understanding of the way language actually works. For a start, it makes the dubious assumption that the terms being criticized are understood by contemporary English speakers as descriptive labels for disability or mental illness: that's what makes them offensive when they're used to disparage people who aren't disabled or mentally ill. It's true that in some cases they did originally denote physical or cognitive impairments. *Dumb*, for instance, meant 'mute, without speech'. But that meaning was superseded long ago by the 'stupid' meaning. No modern clinician treating language impaired patients refers to them as 'dumb'; if I told you I'd met a dumb person you'd assume I meant she was stupid, not that she couldn't speak. In other cases (like *weird(o)*, which comes from the lexicon of magic rather than medicine) there isn't even a historical connection. Calling someone with autism or OCD a weirdo may be insensitive and mean, but it doesn't make *weirdo* an ableist term in the way that, say, the N-word is a racist term.

Do people with disabilities feel insulted by figurative uses of words like *dumb* and *lame*? The short answer is, it depends which disabled people you ask: as usual, there's a range of views within the group. But in this genre of advice, the statement that a word is offensive to a certain group of people is rarely if ever based on any systematic attempt to find out what group members think. Sometimes it becomes painfully obvious that no one from the group has been consulted. In 2023, for instance, the Associated Press style guide (an influential source of language advice for journalists) tweeted a reminder to avoid the definite article in references to ethnic groups such as 'the French'. This advice was mocked by numerous respondents, including the French Embassy in Washington, DC; one tweet asked if the correct expression would be 'people experiencing Frenchness'.

The *Harvard Business Review* piece is also typical of its genre in failing to appreciate that linguistic norms are contextually variable, and that competent communicators need to be able to operate in more than one linguistic register (*register* means, roughly, a variety of language whose characteristics reflect what it's used for and in what social situations). 'Concentrate on why you don't like Trump's policies and skip the personal insults' is good advice for participants in an academic seminar, but it would be odd to use the same register for having an argument with someone in a bar. As for the idea that we could and should get along without disparaging words of any kind, I can only say I've never heard of a language whose vocabulary does not contain such words; communicating disapproval is something people in all cultures use language to do. Social justice activists are no exception: they may not use words like *dumb* and *crazy*, but they certainly don't refrain from accusing, disparaging and shaming people.

This genre of language advice has long been an easy target for both conservative and liberal critics of the radical left, and during the early 2020s, as the 'war on woke' heated up, there were regular outbreaks of public controversy about language guidelines produced at US universities. To readers of a certain age (myself included) these were reminiscent of the 'political correctness gone mad' stories that appeared in newspapers in the early 1990s. But back then newspapers at least had some obligation to check their facts and print a statement from the institution they were criticizing. Today these controversies tend to start on social media, where they can quickly spiral out of control.

In 2023, for instance, the Office for Diversity and Inclusion at Johns Hopkins University published an online glossary of LGBTQ+ terms whose definition of *lesbian* as 'a non-man attracted to non-men' was criticized by, among others, J. K.

Rowling and Martina Navratilova. The university was then deluged with complaints which assumed the glossary represented, and was being enforced as, its official policy. In fact it had no such status: the people in charge of the institution had no idea it even existed until the pile-on faced them with an urgent PR problem. Their response was to take the glossary down, but people continued to share screenshots of the offending definition. Consequently an internal document which in the normal course of events would probably have reached a few hundred people on campus was dissected, debated and denounced by thousands of people around the world.

Something similar had happened in 2021, when Brandeis University's Prevention, Advocacy and Resource Center (PARC) published a guide to 'oppressive language', urging readers to avoid a long list of words and idioms which were said to be traumatizing for victims of violence. One of the expressions its authors criticized (to the surprise of readers who associated it with campus 'snowflakes') was 'trigger warning': the word *trigger*, they explained, would make people think of guns. They also reiterated a suggestion originally made by the animal rights organization PETA, that the idiom 'kill two birds with one stone' should be replaced by 'feed two birds with one scone' (though as critics pointed out, this substitution misses the point: rather than accomplishing two things with one action, you're just giving each bird less food). Other words and phrases to be avoided included *picnic* (which was said to be a reference to lynching[8]), and 'rule of thumb' (allegedly an allusion to an old legal judgment permitting Englishmen to beat their wives so long as the implement they used was no thicker than their thumb[9]).

As with the ableist language piece I discussed earlier, the claim that these expressions were harmful depended on taking figurative language literally and ignoring the fact that language changes. Idioms like 'kill two birds with one stone' are metaphors that have fossilized over time, becoming fixed formulas which speakers no longer connect to the literal meaning they were based on originally. Suggesting that people should stop using these expressions to avoid traumatizing victims of violence is a bit like suggesting we should retire the word *goodbye* (derived from 'God be with you') to avoid offending people who don't believe in a single, or any, god. Historical meanings that contemporary speakers are not aware of do not affect what words and idioms communicate in present-day English. Because of that, as the linguist John McWhorter commented, a lot of PARC's advice was as futile as 'proclaiming that the clouds shall never again move'.[10]

'Futile' is a common description of this enterprise, but what I find most striking about it, and what connects it to dogwhistle politics in the sense I've used that term in this book, is the paranoid way of thinking that underpins it. Those engaged in it see danger everywhere: believing that almost anything we say, whether we realize it or not, could be spreading social evils like racism and violence and causing harm to vulnerable people, they have embarked on a single-minded, never-ending quest to root out the malign messages which are hidden in everyday language. Like the dogwhistle detectives discussed in Chapter 3, these harm-hunters are not deterred by others' scepticism. They are ingenious readers, always looking for new linguistic threats and new reasons why we urgently need to stop saying one thing and start saying another.

Recently, for instance, more radical progressives have stopped saying *homeless* and started saying *unhoused*. Online I've seen people asking what the difference is and being told that *homeless* implies having nowhere to live is just something that happens to some people, whereas *unhoused* makes clear that if you have nowhere to live that's because the authorities have failed in their duty to house you. Unsurprisingly, I've also seen people scoffing at this explanation. But should they be so quick to scoff at it? Though I'm not aware of any evidence that substituting *unhoused* for *homeless* changes perceptions, it's not inconceivable that it might. We've already seen that in some circumstances the replacement of a word with a near-synonym (e.g., *assistance* for *welfare*) can make a measurable difference to people's responses. The old joke about paranoia – 'just because you're paranoid doesn't mean they're *not* out to get you' – has a point: just because some claims about language are implausible and excessive doesn't mean we should assume that every problem activists draw attention to is imaginary, or that every solution they propose is just a futile 'symbolic gesture'.

About fifty years ago, second-wave feminists drew attention to the problem of the 'generic masculine' – the use of grammatically masculine forms to refer to people in general, as in 'the artist must be true to his vision', or 'an effective board of directors needs a strong chairman'. By the mid-1970s the complaint that these terms excluded women was based on more than just political conviction: there was empirical evidence that hearing or reading what some feminists dubbed 'he/man language' overwhelmingly activated mental representations of men. There was also evidence (and today there's even more) which showed that substituting neutral or inclusive terms like *chair* or *his or her* can significantly reduce that tendency.[11] More recent research has demonstrated that linguistic modifications can help to neutralize less obvious kinds of male bias. For instance, you can get more women to apply for a job if you avoid using certain words in the job advertisement – words which in theory are applicable to individuals of either sex, but which in practice have acquired a strong association with masculinity, and so implicitly communicate to many women that the job is not for them. If you don't want to exclude qualified women from your applicant pool you should avoid describing your ideal candidate as, say, 'a self-confident individual who is driven to achieve results' and instead advertise for 'an enthusiastic team-member who is committed to achieving results'.[12] Though it's depressing that this kind of sex-stereotyping still exerts so much influence, knowing that it does can help organizations to do something practical to mitigate the effects.

But while these cases show that changing the language used in particular contexts can make a material (not just symbolic) difference, it's clear if you track such initiatives over time that some are more successful than others. In the case of feminist campaigns against sexist language, for instance, the proposal to replace masculine occupational titles (e.g., *fireman* and *policeman*) with gender-neutral alternatives (e.g., *firefighter* and *police officer*) has been far more successful than the contemporaneous proposal to replace the marital-status-marked titles *Miss* and *Mrs* with a single female title, *Ms*. Whereas *police officer* is now the norm, *Ms* is still a minority choice, and has never come close to replacing *Miss/Mrs*. What this illustrates is that activists can't just impose their preferences by fiat. New ways of using language will not spread very far unless enough people in the wider speech community are receptive to the argument for change. Not everyone needs to be on board, but if most people are sceptical or hostile the new form will not become dominant. This is why documents like the PARC guidelines tend not to accomplish much in practice. Since their recommendations are based on arguments which have little or no currency beyond the subculture where they originated, it's unlikely they'll be followed by people outside that subculture.

But in that case, you might ask, why do people get so exercised about them? The outrage generated by the PARC guidelines (which Brandeis eventually made PARC take down because they were attracting so much negative publicity) was out of all proportion to any effect they were ever likely to have in the wider world. Maybe that shows how much the 'woke' and the anti-'woke' have in common: both believe in the power of language to impose certain ways of thinking on its users, they just differ on which ways of thinking those should be. One side wants to ban language that allegedly promotes racism and violence; the other wants to ban language that allegedly undermines traditional family values. But that raises another question. Critics of what they wrongly took to be the official language policies of Brandeis and Johns Hopkins accused those institutions of using language to indoctrinate their students with pernicious and nonsensical ideas. But if the critics had been able to form the opinion that the guidelines were pernicious nonsense, why did they think students would be incapable of doing the same? This is a feature of Orwell-style language criticism that has always bothered me. Writers who warn that Newspeak or Wokespeak is being used to control people's thoughts are always worried about other people's susceptibility to this tactic, never their own; they can see clearly what the bad guys are up to and explain it to the rest of us. But they never explain what enables them to do this. If language is so powerful, why doesn't its power work on them?

Elitism, authority and exclusion

The substitution of *unhoused* for *homeless* may or may not change perceptions of the people so labelled, but one thing it does do is make *unhoused* into a kind of codeword, signifying that the person who uses it is a member of the in-group that knows *unhoused* is the 'right' word while *homeless* is now 'wrong'. All kinds of in-group language serve this purpose (an obvious non-political example is teenage slang), but in this case the effect is to elevate a highly privileged group of people to the status of authorities on how less privileged people should or shouldn't be talked about. For critics like Musa al-Gharbi that gesture is arrogant, alienating and exclusionary.

The arrogance is perhaps most clearly on display in cases where a group of less privileged people voice objections to the activists' language, saying they don't want to be labelled, for instance, *Latinx*, or *queer*, and are told either that they need to educate themselves – clearly they haven't kept up with the

latest thinking on social justice – or else that they've internal-
ized the prejudice the activists are trying to combat.[13] These
responses, which imply that members of minority groups only
hold the views they do because they don't know any better, are
obviously patronizing, and likely, as some leftist critics have
argued, to alienate people at the sharp end of injustice from the
movements that claim to serve their interests.

Alienation is also manifested in something I mentioned in
Chapter 1 – the reluctance of people with no strong tribal
allegiance to get involved in debates they describe as 'toxic'.
'Toxic' in this context is shorthand for a number of things
people dislike or disapprove of, including extreme polarization, aggressive language and underhand tactics like smearing
opponents. But another thing that's quite often mentioned as
a deterrent to speaking up is the perception of these debates
as linguistic minefields. If you use the 'wrong' words you'll
be branded a bigot, but the 'right' words are obscure and
constantly changing. That isn't an entirely new problem. A
friend of mine who worked for a leftist local council in London
in the 1980s recalls being so worried about using the wrong
language at work meetings that she simply resorted to saying
nothing. But as more forms of identity and inequality have
been brought under the social justice umbrella, and as social
justice has moved onto the agenda of more institutions, new
terms, concepts and distinctions have proliferated, creating
more opportunities for more people to get things wrong.

Though even educated professionals like my friend can be
silenced by their anxieties about using the 'wrong' words, most
progressive critics share Musa al-Gharbi's concern that 'woke'
language is particularly likely to exclude and silence non-elite
groups. Its obscure vocabulary and convoluted phrasing are
often said to make it confusing or incomprehensible to people
with little formal education, low levels of literacy or limited
proficiency in the majority language. But while this argument
is both intuitively plausible and rhetorically powerful (since in

effect it accuses the 'woke' of hypocrisy, of claiming to stand with the most marginalized in society while speaking a language those people can't understand), I think it oversimplifies what is actually a more complex issue.

One problem I have with it is that it seems to equate lacking formal education with lacking the capacity to learn – a form of (class) elitism in its own right. I mentioned in Chapter 1 that I got part of my early political education from old-school leftists. Some of them were working-class men and women who'd left school at the age of fifteen, but that hadn't stopped them becoming fluent in the language of Marxism. They'd learned it not in college courses, but by reading books they borrowed from libraries and attending political education sessions organized by their unions or the small leftist sects they belonged to. Of course, not all working-class people knew this language, but the ones who did acted as mediators, explaining ideas they thought were useful in ways that made sense to the other people they were trying to organize in their workplaces and local communities. Such mediators have always played an important role in progressive social movements. It's unrealistic to think those movements could speak entirely in everyday, jargon-free language: part of their task is to formulate an analysis of the problems they aim to solve, and that will always lead them to come up with concepts, and names for concepts, which the majority of people will initially find obscure. But in most cases that has more do with their unfamiliarity than their intrinsic difficulty; in time, if they serve a purpose, they will be absorbed into everyday language.

Consider, for instance, the word *parenting*. When this gender-neutral term first started to appear regularly in mainstream sources, it was derided both as a grammatical monstrosity ('you can't just make nouns into verbs!' – though in fact it's a feature of English that you can) and as abstruse 'politically correct' jargon which a radical vanguard was trying to impose on everyone else. But over time people stopped perceiving it as abstruse, or indeed political, and it is now completely unremarkable: in contemporary written English it appears ten times more frequently than *mothering*.[14] Is there any reason to think that terms which are currently derided as impenetrable 'woke' jargon, like *BIPOC* and *cishet*, won't make the same journey?

Actually, there might be. As I noted earlier, politically motivated language changes will only become normalized if enough people are receptive to the thinking behind them. *Parenting* was able to move from the radical margins to the mainstream not just because people got used to hearing it, but because it fit with the increasingly widespread belief that taking care of children should ideally be a shared responsibility, involving fathers as well as mothers. For the growing number of people who not only held that belief but had incorporated it into their everyday practice, *parenting* filled a gap by providing a word parents, but particularly fathers, could use to talk about their role.[15] What makes 'woke' innovations different is that in many cases they aren't spreading because they resonate with beliefs that have become widely accepted in society as a whole; rather, their use is being imposed by institutions.

One vehicle for this imposition is the DEI policies which are now embedded in many workplaces and universities. But in addition, activists have adopted a strategy of lobbying influential linguistic 'gatekeepers' – for instance, editors at dictionaries, publishing houses, press agencies, major newspapers and broadcasters – to recognize their preferred terms and, where applicable, prescribe their use as part of the 'house style' writers or speakers have to follow. This top-down approach may speed up the process of familiarizing people with linguistic innovations, but it doesn't necessarily speed up their acceptance; on the contrary, in fact, the effect may be to provoke resistance. One common form this resistance takes is complaints that the new terms are unintelligible, especially to less educated people. But like so many of the claims about language I've examined in this book, that can't always be taken at face value. It may be a strategic move in an argument which has more to do with politics than reading comprehension.

In Britain in recent years there has been considerable resistance to the adoption by institutions of new terminology which has been recommended as 'trans-inclusive'. In the National Health Service, for instance, leaflets and web pages on subjects like menstruation, pregnancy and childbirth, breastfeeding and gynaecological cancers have replaced references to *women* and *mothers* with terms such as 'birthing parent', 'chestfeeding', 'pregnant people' and 'people/anyone with a cervix'. These modifications have been accused not only of symbolically erasing women, but also of putting women's health at risk by rendering important information opaque – particularly, once again, to women who are less educated, less literate or less proficient in English.[16] The claim that these groups of women find the new trans-inclusive terms confusing or incomprehensible has appeared in sources that range from opinion pieces[17] to academic journal articles with scores of footnotes.[18] But even the academics present it as just obvious common sense: they cite no research, done by themselves or anyone else, that has tested the claim directly. That doesn't mean we can just dismiss the claim; as the saying goes, absence of evidence is not evidence of absence. But the amount of heat this argument has generated makes the apparent dearth of evidence surprising. As well as shedding light on whether there's a problem, if there is, research would give us a clearer idea of what it is, how serious it is, and who is affected by it.

The answers to those questions may be less obvious than is generally assumed. Not all the terms that provoke heated debate seem equally likely to cause the degree of difficulty that's been alleged: if you know the words *pregnant* and *people*, for instance, decoding 'pregnant people' is straightforward. You may not understand *why* that phrase is being used, but that's a different kind of problem from having no idea what it means.

Other formulas, however, may cause more difficulty than has been assumed, because the issue isn't only or primarily the words. 'Pregnant people' is reasonably transparent because all it does is substitute *people* for *women* (who are of course also people): there's nothing novel or obscure about the basic concept of people being pregnant. But there are other words and phrases which you will struggle to make sense of unless you can relate them to certain unstated propositions which the terms presuppose are part of your stock of background knowledge. And while it's true that all of us are continually adding to our background knowledge, we don't all start from the same point or have access to the same range of sources. Genuine comprehension problems can arise when ideas which are not, in fact, universally familiar are assumed to be common knowledge.

Uncommon knowledge and the 2021 Census

In 2021 the decennial Census for England and Wales, a regular data-gathering exercise carried out by the Office for National Statistics (ONS), included a new question about gender identity which was intended to give researchers, planners and policy-makers some basic information about the size, composition and geographical distribution of the two countries' trans and nonbinary population. To elicit the relevant information the ONS used a slightly adapted version of a question developed some years earlier by a trans activist group. The original wording had been 'Is the gender you identify with the same as your gender assigned at birth?' The ONS substituted 'registered' for 'assigned' and 'sex' for the second occurrence of 'gender', ending up with 'Is the gender you identify with the same as your sex registered at birth?' This did eliminate one possible source of confusion (the phrase 'assigned at birth'), but it still assumed that everyone filling in the census would know what it meant to 'identify with' a gender, and it ignored the fact that for many English speakers *sex* and *gender* mean the same thing (both are used to refer to a person's sex, but since *sex* also means 'copulation', many people use *gender* simply as a 'polite' alternative). The census question presupposed, in short, that the whole population was familiar with what the sociologist Michael Biggs describes as 'a discourse on gender that had recently circulated among the professional-managerial class'.[19]

Biggs carried out an analysis of responses to this question, and concluded that it had produced flawed and misleading data. In his judgment only 80,000 of the 262,000 responses the ONS had classified as indicating a trans identity did not raise any questions about the validity of that classification. In many cases the respondent had ticked the 'no' box (i.e., said their gender was different from their birth-registered sex), but then written in a gender identity that was the same as their birth-registered sex. What these anomalous responses meant was impossible to know for sure, but a suspiciously high proportion of the people who had produced them also reported that English (or Welsh, in Wales) was not their home language and that they spoke it poorly. Though only 10 per cent of all census respondents were non-native speakers, they accounted for nearly 30 per cent of those who were recorded as trans. Also overrepresented were people (of all ethnicities) who had few or no educational qualifications. In Biggs's view the most plausible explanation for these patterns was that large numbers of people in these categories had unintentionally given misleading answers because they didn't understand the question. If that were true, though, it would make the overall figures the census had produced on the size, composition and location of the trans population invalid.

Biggs was not alone in doubting their validity. The Organization for Statistics Regulation agreed that the figures raised serious questions. After carrying out a review it downgraded them from 'accredited official statistics' to 'official statistics in development'.[20] This was a blow to the reputation of the ONS, which had never had a census finding de-accredited before; it was also something of a surprise, since the mistake that led to it is not one you would expect trained and experienced survey designers to make. It's especially puzzling that they made it in this case, because when they chose the question there was already evidence from earlier pilot tests that people who were not trans found it 'very confusing'. But the question had strong support from the trans groups the ONS had consulted, which had repeatedly rejected simpler alternatives. 'Are you transgender?', for instance, was not acceptable because some trans people might not identify with that label; wordings like 'do you consider yourself . . . / think of yourself as . . .' were said to be offensive because they implied that a respondent's identity was a matter of opinion or belief rather than a fact. Quite ordinary turns of phrase were persistently read as either microaggressions belittling trans people or dogwhistles to those who disputed their existence – another example of the paranoid style of interpretation.

A purely 'professional' response to this feedback might have been something like 'we understand your reservations, but to get accurate information about your community we need a question that's clear to the majority of respondents, and we already know most people find the question you prefer confusing'. But records of the ONS's discussions suggest that they were more concerned about how trans and nonbinary people would react to the question than about how it would be interpreted by other groups of respondents. In effect, both they and the activists they consulted put the symbolic function of language above its communicative function. Though both parties had a clear interest in gathering accurate data on gender identity, both ultimately took the view that it was more important for the language used in the question to display respect for trans people's identities, beliefs and feelings than for it to make what it was asking clear to a large and diverse population.

Others colluded in turning this part of the census into a culture war battleground. While it's likely that most of the anomalous responses noted by Michael Biggs came from people who had inadvertently given the wrong answer to the gender identity question because they didn't understand it, some probably came from trans people whose written-in gender identity matched their birth-registered sex because they had deliberately given the wrong answer to the sex question (i.e., ignored the instruction to report the sex recorded on their birth certificate and instead reported their current gender). There were also people who treated the gender identity question as an opportunity to air their objections to the concept of gender identity: some ticked the 'no' box and then wrote in responses like 'no gender' or 'gender free' (a gesture whose effect, ironically, was to get them classified as trans). All sides in this battle seemed to have lost sight of the fact that it served no one's interests for the data gap the census was meant to fill to be filled with unreliable and misleading data. By refusing to act like cooperative communicators, making a good-faith effort to retrieve the intended meaning of the questions and answer them accordingly, they all contributed to exactly that outcome.

Dogwhistle politics and the 'worst-faith reading of everything'

I have said many times in this book that human linguistic communication is imperfect. But more and more, I find myself asking: does it really have to be this bad? Why is there so much paranoia and bad faith? Why are so many people so insistent on looking, not for the meaning another person is trying to communicate, but for something in the form of the message that can be used to accuse them of malfeasance? Is anyone even interested in communicating any more?

I'm not the only person who has asked that question. In January 2025 I stumbled across a thread on X where a group of people I didn't know were swapping stories about the intolerance that had caused them to become disillusioned with the left. While a couple of them maintained that the left had always been intolerant, most seemed to think that even in the relatively recent past its intolerance had been less extreme. One suggested that 2016, the year of Trump and Brexit, had been a turning point. After that, this writer recalled,

> It wasn't enough to just believe the right things. Silence was violence. You had to call people out and ostracize them for having the wrong views. So I had friends who proudly reported kicking visiting relatives out to go and stay in a hotel because they'd said something inadvertently 'racist' or 'transphobic' over breakfast. And I put those in quotes because the movement also demands that you give worst-faith readings of everything. You must see bigotry everywhere so you can stamp it out.

That phrase 'worst-faith readings of everything' leapt out at me, because it seemed to capture some of the essential features of dogwhistle politics in the sense I've been using that term – to label a particular way of thinking about the politics of language and communication. This way of thinking is rooted in mistrust and fear; it assumes that bigotry is everywhere and that anything anyone says may contain a coded message of hate. It encourages people to be incurious and defensive, listening only for what confirms their preconceptions and discarding anything else. It is intolerant and punitive, requiring in-group members and 'allies' to demonstrate their purity not only by calling out others' transgressions, but also by engaging in continuous self-policing (and if that fails, self-abasement: celebrities with 'woke' followings have had to master the art of the public apology accompanied by promises to 'educate myself' and 'do better'[21]).

What practitioners of this kind of politics are engaged in is a form of what I have elsewhere called 'verbal hygiene': they are trying to impose order on language as a proxy for imposing order on a less tractable social reality.[22] That is an ingrained human habit; in some form or other it seems to exist in every culture, and its history stretches back to antiquity. Neither inherently reactionary nor inherently radical, it has been used for all kinds of purposes by people with all kinds of beliefs – but it has rarely produced the intended results. Most verbal hygiene projects overstate not only the power of language to change the world on its own, but also the power of any one group in a society to control the way language is used. Even in societies where the powerful can exert strict control over the language of public discourse, the language that lives in people's minds, and in their everyday conversations, is a different matter. That point was demonstrated dramatically after the collapse of communism in Central and Eastern Europe. Linguistic norms that had been publicly enforced for nearly half a century, like the use of the address term *Comrade* and the naming of authoritarian institutions as 'the People's', were quickly abandoned and replaced with pre-communist norms. The erasure of these older conventions from the language of public life had evidently depended more on coercive pressure – in particular, people's fear of the consequences of deviating from the regime's prescribed vocabulary – than on any popular enthusiasm for what the new terms represented.

'Woke' verbal hygienists may not have the same power as the communist regimes of twentieth-century Europe, but to the extent they have managed to enforce individual and institutional compliance with their linguistic norms they too have relied to a considerable extent on fear; to induce it they have been not just willing but eager to harness the power of the state, the law and the online mob. And I think it is clear that their embrace of these methods has done serious damage to the progressive cause. It has produced a large number of people like the ones in the X thread I quoted above, who have deserted the left and are now politically homeless, and prompted others to support right-wing populists who promise to put a stop to 'woke' authoritarianism. As I noted earlier, what that promise has turned out to mean in practice is just replacing 'woke' language policing with a right-wing version of the same thing. Yet the 'woke' leftists who now complain about the authoritarian and punitive nature of the Trump administration's word-banning, or Reform UK's recent edict prohibiting rainbow flags on council buildings,[23] seem to have nothing to say about the obvious fact that these tactics are part of their playbook too.

Perhaps if they were pressed they would say there is no moral equivalence between the actions of a resistance movement and the actions of the regime it is trying to overthrow – a defence in the spirit of the tradition of language criticism I talked about in Chapter 1, which frames language as a weapon used by the powerful to maintain and legitimize their power. That framing resonates with many people because it is felt to capture something true and important about both the modern workings of power and the political significance of language. But while I don't dispute that assessment of the basic idea, I have serious reservations about the extreme interpretation which has come to dominate the thinking and practice of the progressive left.

One obvious problem is that this way of thinking, and the kinds of activism which go with it, tend to diminish rather than increase popular support for progressive causes. 'Woke' activists have adopted, in the name of resistance to right-wing authoritarianism, practices which are themselves so authoritarian that many people are repelled by them; the effect has been to divide the left and give its enemies an easy target. But in addition, I think it's a problem that the idea of language as a weapon wielded by the powerful has become so dominant as to eclipse all other ways of thinking about what language does and why it matters. As more and more emphasis is put on stamping out ways of using words which are said to be oppressive, manipulative and harmful, there is less and less space for the idea that language is a resource which enables us, despite our differences and conflicts, to connect with one another, to find common ground and to cooperate in pursuit of goals we share. To my mind, that more positive way of thinking about the power of language is as important for progressive politics as the other. The danger is that if we cannot reclaim it, we will stay where we are now – arguing about symbols on the sidelines or purging dissenters from our own ranks, while those with real power make decisions that oppress and endanger us all.

Acknowledgements

For their interest, support and comments on work in progress I am grateful to Meryl Altman, Andrew Beach, Elizabeth Frazer, Deborah Georgiou, Carl Ginet, Sally McConnell-Ginet, Miriam Meyerhoff and Arlene Oak. Thanks also to the anonymous reviewers, and to Elise Heslinga at Polity for the idea that turned into this book.

Notes

1 The Rise of Dogwhistle Politics

1 Since some readers of a draft of this chapter thought I must be making these examples up, let me say for the record that all of them are real. The scarf and the cuddly toy will be discussed in Chapter 3; on the images of classical buildings see Beorn, W. W. (2024) 'The "classical culture" social media accounts that look like dogwhistles for the far right', *Byline Supplement*, 5 May, https://www.bylinesupplement.com/p/the-classical-culture-social-media.

2 The evidence for these claims, which I discuss further in Chapter 3, comes from two large collections of published texts: Google Books and the newspaper database LexisNexis.

3 This description is taken from a thread on X which I came across by chance in early 2025; I discuss it more fully in Chapter 6.

4 Morin, W. (1988) 'Behind the numbers: confessions of a pollster', *Washington Post*, 16 October.

5 A history and analysis of this phenomenon in the US between 1968 and 2013 is Haney-López, I. (2014) *Dogwhistle Politics: How Coded Racial Appeals Have Reinvented Racism and Wrecked the Middle Class.* Oxford University Press (an updated edition is due to appear in 2025).

6 See Perlstein, R. (2012) 'Exclusive: Lee Atwater's infamous 1981 interview on the Southern Strategy', *The Nation*, 13 November.
7 Some writers might quibble with this formulation, arguing that politicians who employ racist dogwhistles do not necessarily subscribe to racist beliefs themselves; the point is rather that even if they are not racists they strategically appeal to racist beliefs for their own political gain. Ian Haney-López makes this argument about Bill Clinton, for example. See Haney-López, *Dogwhistle Politics*, p. 113.
8 Here and elsewhere I have chosen to use the general term *message* rather than, say, *statement* or *expression* because it is neutral as to the medium or means of communication, covering not just cases involving language, but also (to give some examples that will crop up later in this book) visual images, gestures, numbers and objects.
9 George W. Bush has featured in many academic discussions of dogwhistling because of his habit of quoting evangelical Christian texts: according to those who analysed these allusions as dogwhistles, their purpose was to assure religious conservatives of his commitment to advancing their political agenda without making that obvious to other listeners.
10 Perlman, M. (2016) 'Dog whistle, dumpster fire', *Columbia Journalism Review*, 25 July, https://www.cjr.org/language_cor ner/dog_whistle_dumpster_fire.php.
11 Contemporary examples of the use of coded messaging outside the domain of politics include commercial advertising and corporate PR; historically the technique of constructing messages to be picked up by readers 'in the know' while passing others by was often employed in scientific and philosophical writing as a strategy for avoiding censorship by state or religious authorities.
12 Critics of Cleon's demagogy were not social egalitarians but aristocrats defending the traditions of Athenian democracy (from which they benefited). Comparisons with our own time have been made, however. Cleon features as a character in the video-

game *Assassin's Creed Odyssey*, where he is given the line 'I will make Athens great again.'

13 Klemperer, V. (2002 [1957]) *The Language of the Third Reich.* Bloomsbury, p. 15.

14 Herman, E. and Chomsky, N. (2002) *Manufacturing Consent: The Political Economy of the Mass Media.* Pantheon Books.

15 Lakoff, G. (1990) *Don't Think of an Elephant! Know Your Values and Frame the Debate.* Chelsea Green Publishing.

16 See van Leeuwen, T. (2006) 'Critical discourse analysis', in *The Encyclopedia of Language and Linguistics*, 2nd edn, ed. K. Brown. Elsevier, pp. 290–4.

17 Authoritarian 'strongman' leaders elected around the world between 2010 and the present include Hungary's Viktor Orbán, India's Narendra Modi, Turkey's Recep Tayyip Erdoğan, Jair Bolsonaro in Brazil, Rodrigo Duterte in the Philippines and Donald Trump in the US. European political parties with fascist ancestry include the Austrian Freedom Party, the Brothers of Italy and the National Rally in France; parties formed more recently on a platform of ethnic nationalism and hostility to immigration include Alternative für Deutschland in Germany, the Sweden Democrats, and the various parties which have been led by Nigel Farage in the UK (his latest vehicle, Reform UK, won several parliamentary seats in the 2024 General Election).

18 The political rise of Donald Trump and the events of his first presidential term have had, by her own account, a major influence on the most recent work of the philosopher and noted dogwhistle scholar Jennifer Saul. See Saul, J. (2023) *Dogwhistles and Figleaves.* Oxford University Press. There have also been some detailed analyses of Trump's rhetoric by sociolinguists and linguistic anthropologists. See contributions to McIntosh, J. and Mendoza-Denton, N. (eds.) (2020) *Language in the Trump Era.* Cambridge University Press; and Sclafani, J. (2018) *Talking Donald Trump.* Routledge.

19 Starmer's actual words were: 'Point out that the view on the ground is very different to that from his private jet, and he says

you're talking the country down. He just doesn't get it, he doesn't get what a cost-of-living crisis feels like. He doesn't know any schools where kids no longer turn up, and he doesn't understand what it's like to wait for a hospital appointment. Doesn't the country deserve so much better than a Prime Minister who simply doesn't get Britain?'

20 See Karlsson, C.-J. (2024) 'Divided we stand: the rise of political animosity', *Knowable Magazine*, 19 August, https://knowablema gazine.org/content/article/society/2024/latest-research-what-ca uses-political-polarization.

21 See Murray, M. and Marquez, A. (2023) 'Here's what's driving America's increasing political polarization', *NBC News*, 15 June, https://www.nbcnews.com/meet-the-press/meetthepressblog /s-s-driving-americas-increasing-political-polarization-rcna8 9559.

22 This argument is made, for instance, in Klein, N. (2023) *Doppelganger: A Trip into the Mirror World*. Allen Lane.

23 The belief that culture, broadly defined, is an important site of political struggle is central to the thought of canonical Marxist theorists like Antonio Gramsci and the members of the Frankfurt School (the original 'cultural Marxists'), as well as more recent figures like Pierre Bourdieu and Stuart Hall.

24 I am somewhat reluctant to use this term, because today it is almost always used as an insult: it has been described as both a dogwhistle and a slur. Historically it was a positive label, used by black radicals in the US to describe someone who had become conscious of racial oppression and committed to resisting it, but today non-pejorative uses are rare. Since I am even less sympathetic to the conservatives who use it as an insult than to the people they're insulting (I'm critical of the 'woke' left, but I share its basic commitment to social justice), I did consider whether there was a less loaded term I could substitute. But I came to the conclusion there wasn't: other labels either don't distinguish this strand of progressive politics clearly from others, or else they are obscure without being any less disparaging. My compromise will

be to put 'woke' in scare quotes, as a reminder that its meaning is contested.

25 Contributions to this literature include DeBoer, F. (2023) *How Elites Ate the Social Justice Movement*. Simon & Schuster; al-Gharbi, M. (2024) *We Have Never Been Woke*. Princeton University Press; Mounk, Y. (2023) *The Identity Trap*. Allen Lane; Neiman, S. (2023) *Left Is Not Woke*. Polity; Özkýrýmlý, U. (2023) *Cancelled: The Left Way Back from Woke*. Polity; and Táíwò, O. O. (2022) *Elite Capture*. Pluto Press.

26 Mounk, *The Identity Trap*, p. 67.

27 DeBoer, *How Elites Ate the Social Justice Movement*, p. 67.

28 In *We Have Never Been Woke*, Musa al-Gharbi dubs this group 'symbolic capitalists'. The term alludes to the social theorist Pierre Bourdieu's concept of 'symbolic capital', a set of intangible assets (e.g., qualifications, skills, tastes, ways of speaking) acquired by a society's elite class via socialization and formal education. Symbolic capital can be exchanged for financial capital (typically in the form of a professional salary), but even if it doesn't make its possessor rich it can still confer status or prestige. Al-Gharbi's argument is that 'wokeness' is a form of symbolic capital used by elite individuals to compete for status with one another.

29 De Boer, *How Elites Ate the Social Justice Movement*, p. 75.

30 Here I'm quoting Henninger, D. (2017) 'The free speech wars', *Wall Street Journal*, 11 October. The full sentence in which the words appear is 'these students think, or have been taught to think, that free speech is just a dog whistle for the alt-right'. Though it might be objected that this writer is putting words in the students' mouths, there have been other reports of these words being used by 'woke' campus activists (for examples, see, e.g., https://www.youtube.com/watch?v=9MrajtcYjJc). It is undeniable that the cause of free speech has been seized on by right-wing authoritarians who do not in reality support it as a convenient stick to beat the left with, but what has made this an effective tactic is, precisely, 'woke' attacks on free

speech as something that only serves the interests of racists and bigots. The way that argument has been appropriated by the Trump administration and used to justify the suppression of speech the right disagrees with will be discussed further in Chapter 6.

31 An account of Gamergate, and of the tactics of the alt-right more generally, is given in Nagle, A. (2017) *Kill All Normies: Online Culture Wars from 4Chan and Tumblr to Trump and the Alt-Right.* Zero Books.

32 For a summary of recent trends relating to the removal of books from both school and public libraries in the US, see American Library Association, 'Book ban data', https://www.ala.org/bboo ks/book-ban-data. For the UK there appears to be no comparable, centralized source of data, but a small survey conducted in 2024 by the pressure group Index on Censorship revealed that some schools have been pressured (most commonly by religious conservative groups) to remove library books, particularly titles on LGBT themes. See Dancey-Downs, K. (2024) 'Banned: school librarians shushed over LGBT+ books', https://www.index oncensorship.org/2024/08/banned-school-librarians-shushed -over-lgbt-books. In both countries there is concern that this overt censorship may also be prompting librarians to engage in 'soft' censorship by choosing not to purchase titles that might be challenged.

33 One recent example of (attempted) decommissioning is the decision of the publisher Picador to drop the poet and teacher Kate Clanchy after one of her books was attacked for allegedly using racist language (I say 'attempted' because Clanchy did eventually find another publisher). A widely publicized case of sanitizing is a new edition of the late Roald Dahl's children's books in which the original text has been rewritten to remove racist, sexist and fatphobic language. There have also been campaigns to block the publication of forthcoming titles (e.g., an academic monograph on gender critical feminism which the campaigners obviously couldn't have read before demanding its cancellation), and

cases where employees at publishing houses have lobbied their employer to cancel a book whose author they disapproved of. Though I am not aware of any case in which this pressure has succeeded in preventing publication, there is concern that such campaigns will have a chilling effect, deterring editors from commissioning potentially controversial titles.

34 See Powell, M. (2021) 'Once a bastion of free speech, the ACLU faces an identity crisis', *New York Times*, 6 June.

35 This is an area in which one must be cautious about generalizing, because the law differs significantly in different countries and jurisdictions (which are not always the same thing: in the UK the laws in force in England and Wales may differ from those in Scotland and Northern Ireland, while Australia, Canada and the US have state or provincial laws as well as national/federal ones). However, there does seem to be a general trend towards more active regulation of hate speech.

36 Hains, T. (2024) 'John Kerry tells WEF: our First Amendment stands as a major block against hammering disinformation out of existence', *Real Clear Politics*, 29 September, https://www.realclearpolitics.com/video/2024/09/29/john_kerry_tells_wef_our_first_amendment_stands_as_a_major_block_against_hammering_disinformation_out_of_existence.html.

37 Research has shown that people habitually overestimate the extent of the political differences between their own 'tribe' and the opposing one, and believe extreme ideological positions to be more widespread among their opponents than they actually are. See, e.g., Druckman, J. N., Klar, S., Krupnikov, Y., Levendusky, M. and Ryan, J. N. (2022) '(Mis)estimating affective polarization', *The Journal of Politics* 84.2, pp. 1106–1117.

38 See Cameron, D. (2012 [1995]) *Verbal Hygiene*. Routledge.

2 Understanding Dogwhistles

1 Austin, J. L. (1961) *How To Do Things with Words*. Clarendon Press.

2 Grice, H. P. (1975) 'Logic and conversation', in *Syntax and*

Semantics, Vol. 3: Speech Acts, ed. P. Cole and J. L. Morgan. Academic Press, pp. 41–58.

3 Saul, *Dogwhistles and Figleaves*.

4 Quaranto, A. (2022) 'Dog whistles, covertly coded speech, and the practices that enable them', *Synthese* 200.4, pp. 1–34.

5 Mendelberg, T. (2001) *The Race Card: Campaign Strategy, Implicit Messages, and the Norm of Equality*. Princeton University Press.

6 In other places other terms may do the same job as *inner city* in the US. In France, *banlieue* ('suburb') has similar racial/racist connotations, reflecting the fact that large numbers of people of North African ancestry live in suburbs located on the peripheries of major cities.

7 *Inner city* appears to have started out as a polite alternative to older, more pejorative terms (e.g., *ghetto*). For instance, in 1972 the sociolinguist William Labov published a collection of his work on African American English (AAE) under the title *Language in the Inner City*. Since one aim of this work was explicitly anti-racist – to debunk the belief that AAE was a 'primitive' and 'impoverished' dialect – it's highly unlikely he would have chosen a title that was thought at the time to have racist associations.

8 Hurwitz, J. and Peffley, M. (2005) 'Playing the race card in the post-Willie Horton era: the impact of racialized code words on support for punitive crime policy', *Public Opinion Quarterly* 69.1, pp. 99–112.

9 See Stanley, J. (2015) *How Propaganda Works*. Oxford University Press; Quaranto, A. and Stanley, J. (2023) 'Propaganda', in *Routledge Handbook of Social and Political Philosophy of Language*, ed. J. Khoo and R. K. Sterken. Routledge, pp. 125–46.

10 Goodin, R. and Saward, M. (2005) 'Dog whistles and democratic mandates', *The Political Quarterly* 76, pp. 471–6.

11 Valentino, N. A., Neuner, F. G. and Vandenbroek, L. M. (2018) 'The changing norms of racial political rhetoric and the end of racial priming', *The Journal of Politics* 80.3, pp. 757–71.

12 Cohen, N. (2009) 'How the BNP's far-right journey ends up on primetime TV', *Guardian*, 18 October.

13 Tillyris, D. (2024) 'Dogwhistling and democracy', *The British Journal of Politics and International Relations* 26.4, pp. 1015–32.

14 The text of the letter and a list of signatories can be found at https://docs.google.com/document/d/17ZqWl5grm_F5Kn_0Oa rY9Q2jlOnk200PvhM5e3isPvY/edit?tab=t.0.

15 Saul, *Dogwhistles and Figleaves*, p. 60.

16 The question may also arise of whether the sender knew, or should have known, that the message was likely to be perceived by some recipients as bigoted. If so, sending it anyway may be seen as an act of culpable negligence (in Chapter 5 I'll discuss a couple of cases where this has been an issue). Either way, though, it's the sender's thoughts and actions that people typically focus on when making judgments.

17 Mounk, Y. (2020) 'Stop firing the innocent', *The Atlantic*, 27 June.

18 Stetler, H. (2024) 'Stop using Jews to launder Marine Le Pen's image: an interview with Simon Assoun', *Jacobin*, 7 April.

19 See, for instance, Strangio, C. (2018) 'The "biological sex" dog-whistle and another unconstitutional assault on trans existence', *Into*, 16 May, https://www.intomore.com/impact/the-biological -sex-dogwhistle-and-another-unconstitutional-assault-on-trans -existence.

20 Brockes, E. (2017) 'Who's taking the fight to Donald Trump? It's Dictionary Guy', *Guardian*, 26 January.

21 Trans people in Britain gained the right to change their legal sex in 2004, but applicants had to meet various conditions (such as having a medical diagnosis of gender dysphoria) which activists considered onerous and demeaning. The proposal to drop these requirements and move to self-ID attracted stronger opposition than most politicians expected, and there has so far been no change in the law. A self-ID bill was passed by the Scottish Parliament in 2022, but its implementation was blocked by the UK government.

22 BBC News (2018) 'Woman billboard removed after transphobia row', 26 September, https://www.bbc.co.uk/news/uk-45650462.

23 The meanings of words are not non-negotiable, as we see from the fact that they change over time. The results of that process will eventually be reflected in dictionaries; for instance, in the last decade many or most dictionaries have modified their definitions of *marriage* to acknowledge the existence of the same-sex variety, though religious conservative opponents of equal marriage had lobbied both legislators and lexicographers using the argument that the word *marriage* means 'the union of a man and a woman'. In that case the claim that 'words have non-negotiable meanings' was rightly dismissed by progressives: it is absurd to suppose that what happens in social and political reality either is or should be determined by the current dictionary definition of a word. Negotiations about the meaning of *woman* are ongoing, both in life and in lexicography: since the 2018 billboard controversy at least one dictionary (the Cambridge English Dictionary) has added a definition based on self-identified gender rather than sex ('an adult who lives and identifies as female/male though they may have been said to have a different sex at birth') to its entries for both *woman* and *man*.

24 I cannot, of course, guarantee that no such examples exist in any source, but the trawling I did for this book turned up none. When conservatives do accuse leftists of dogwhistling they generally seem to use the term in reference to the same forms of prejudice it's most associated with in leftist usage; as we've already seen, for instance, British Conservative MPs accused Keir Starmer of racist dogwhistling and right-wing commentators in France accused Jean-Luc Mélenchon of antisemitic dogwhistling.

3 Dogwhistles Everywhere: How the Concept Has Evolved

1 Haslam, N. (2016) 'Concept creep: psychology's expanding concepts of harm and pathology', *Psychological Inquiry* 27.1, p. 1.

2 Some readers may wonder why I've chosen newspapers over

more 'modern' news sources. Part of the answer is practical: I wanted a searchable archive that covered the whole of the period of interest. But newspapers have other advantages for my purposes: they contain large quantities of reporting and commentary on current political events, and though print sales have fallen steeply in the digital era, their online editions still reach large numbers of people. A 2023 survey found that almost half of all UK adults – and a higher proportion of those over thirty-five – list a newspaper among the news sources they consult most frequently. The most popular news sources overall were the news websites of the BBC and Sky, along with online editions of two newspapers, the *Guardian* and the *Mail*. See Majid, A. (2023) 'Where do Britons get their news?' *Press Gazette*, 12 April, https://pressgazette.co.uk/media-audience-and-business-data/media_metrics/traditional-outlets-still-top-uk-news-sources-survey.

3 In the UK (and some other parts of Europe), anti-immigrant prejudice is not exclusively a white prejudice against non-white incomers. In the 2010s, a lot of anti-immigrant hostility targeted white (and largely Christian) workers from Poland, Romania and other parts of Central/Eastern Europe, who had exercised their free movement rights after their countries of origin joined the EU. The Britons who opposed this arrangement, and voted to leave the EU for that reason, included some non-white citizens whose families had originally come to the UK as immigrants from South Asia, Africa or the Caribbean.

4 I used LexisNexis: I began by searching all English-language newspapers to gauge the currency of *dogwhistle* across the anglophone world, but then concentrated mostly on a subsample of items that had appeared in British national, regional and local newspapers, which I used to look at broad, decade-by-decade trends in the frequency with which the term appeared and the subject matter of articles containing it.

5 Though the items I cite or quote from X/Twitter are all public, I have chosen not to identify their authors. I will in future

refer to the source as Twitter or X depending on the date of the post/tweet under discussion: the rebranding of Twitter as X following its acquisition by Elon Musk took place in July 2023.

6 Cottom, T. M. (2024) 'On cat ladies, mama bears and "Momala"', *New York Times*, 19 August.

7 See Ingram, D. (2024) 'Elon Musk's rightward turn includes a fringe fascination: civil war', *NBC News*, 17 August, https://www .nbcnews.com/tech/internet/elon-musk-predicting-civil-war- europe-nearly-year-rcna165469.

8 The widespread sharing of this definition prompted a series of edits to the Wikipedia entry for 'Stochastic terrorism'. What I've quoted is the version most people shared, which was live until 7 August 2024; it differs in several respects from the version which is live at the time of writing, but it can still be viewed at https:// en.wikipedia.org/w/index.php?title=Stochastic_terrorism&oldi d=1239180596.

9 Matharu, H. (2024) 'The politics of Farage and Reform is no joke of a matter – the established media must learn its lessons and start holding them to account', *Byline Times*, 28 June, https:// bylinetimes.com/2024/06/28/the-politics-of-farage-and-reform -is-no-joke-of-a-matter-the-established-media-must-learn-its -lessons-and-start-holding-them-to-account.

10 This is not a direct quotation but a constructed dialogue based on the account given by the X-user who described Tice as dogwhistling.

11 Saul, *Dogwhistles and Figleaves*, p. 63.

12 In their own time the suffragettes (i.e., members of the Women's Social and Political Union – most supporters of votes for women called themselves 'suffragists', but the *Daily Mail* nicknamed the WSPU 'suffragettes', using the feminine diminutive to belittle them, and they decided to 'reclaim' the intended insult by adopt- ing the label themselves) were far from uncontroversial. They were seen as extreme and divisive even inside the suffrage move- ment: their radical tactics, which included the use of violence,

were deplored by more moderate campaigners. But later popular accounts, coloured by the modern perception of their cause as self-evidently just, have often glossed over the more contentious aspects of their approach, and the effect has been to make them appear more 'respectable' and middle-of-the-road than they really were.

4 'An Offence to Be Offensive': Dogwhistle Politics and the Policing of Speech

1 Mounk, 'Stop firing the innocent'.

2 Sarkisian, J. (2020) 'A best-selling children's author was sacked by her publishers after tweeting her support for JK Rowling', *Business Insider*, 6 July, https://www.businessinsider.com/gilli an-philip-childrens-author-sacked-tweeting-support-jk-rowling -2020-7.

3 Wright, J. (2020) 'Cambridge students demand Labour politician loses his college porter job after he resigned from council in pro-test against pro-transgender motion', *Daily Mail*, 30 November.

4 An employment tribunal in Britain is a court which hears cases brought by employees against employers for allegedly breaching their rights at work. Decisions are made by a panel chaired by a judge, and if employers are found to have been at fault they may be directed to pay the claimant damages. In this case the tribunal awarded damages against both the employer and the regulator; in the regulator's case these were 'exemplary damages', since the tribunal took the view that its treatment of the social worker constituted a serious abuse of its power to regulate the profession.

5 Connelly, T. (2021) 'Abertay Uni law student faces disciplinary action over "offensive" gender comments during online class', *Legal Cheek*, 24 May, https://www.legalcheek.com/2021/05/aber tay-uni-law-student-faces-disciplinary-action-over-offensive -gender-comments-during-online-class.

6 Brown, S. (2024) 'Exeter University student disciplined for saying "veganism is stupid" in his own bedroom', *Devon Live*, 23 April,

https://www.devonlive.com/news/devon-news/university-exet
er-student-disciplined-saying-9242271.

7 'Crown drops transphobia case against Marion Millar', *Scottish Legal News*, 29 October, https://www.scottishlegal.com/articles /crown-drops-transphobia-case-against-marion-millar.

8 Pollard, C. (2023) 'Retired social worker, 73, is quizzed in her own home by hate-crime police for taking a photo of a STICKER that said: "Keep males out of women-only spaces"', *Daily Mail*, 2 September.

9 The protected status of gender critical beliefs was established in 2021 by the judgment of the Employment Appeal Tribunal in the case of Maya Forstater, who had lost her position at a global development think tank because she expressed the beliefs in question on social media. See https://www.gov.uk/employment -appeal-tribunal-decisions/maya-forstater-v-cgd-europe-and-ot hers-ukeat-slash-0105-slash-20-slash-joj.

10 The term is said to have been coined by the *New York Times* writer Ross Douthat in 2015, but the thing itself goes back much further. One famous example is Coca-Cola's 'Hilltop' TV ad featuring the song 'I'd Like To Teach the World To Sing', a hymn to racial harmony and world peace: it was aired in 1971, only a few years after the end of racial segregation and while the US was still fighting the Vietnam War.

11 Quoted in Webber, A. (2024) 'Social worker harassed over gender critical beliefs wins 58K', *Personnel Today*, 29 April, https://www .personneltoday.com/hr/social-worker-harassed-over-gender-cr itical-beliefs-wins-58k.

12 The researchers Ruth Birchall and Jo Phoenix have compiled a full record of 'secular' claims of gender critical belief discrimination (i.e., cases where the claimant's beliefs were held for non-religious reasons) heard by employment tribunals between 2021 and 2024. Their analysis shows that these claims have been upheld in over 80 per cent of cases, whereas in belief discrimination cases generally only about 3 per cent of claims succeed. Apart from the social work department and the regulator already mentioned, the

organizations which have lost tribunal cases brought by gender critical employees include universities, charities, government departments, a Barristers' chambers, a publishing consultancy, the UK Council for Psychotherapy and Arts Council England. See Birchall, R. and Phoenix, J. (2024) *Don't Get Caught Out: A Summary of Gender Critical Belief Discrimination Employment Tribunal Judgments.* School of Law, Reading University, https://centaur.reading.ac.uk/118472/8/Dont%20Get%20Caught%20Out%20final%20%28002%29.pdf.

13 Lukianoff, G. and Haidt, J. (2018) *The Coddling of the American Mind: How Good Intentions and Bad Ideas Are Setting Up a Generation For Failure.* Penguin.

14 As with 'wokeness', a lot of commentary on 'victim culture' falls into the category of unevidenced opinion, but there have been more serious attempts to investigate it as a sociological phenomenon. See for instance Campbell, B. and Manners, J. (2018) *The Rise of Victimhood Culture: Microaggressions, Safe Spaces and the New Culture Wars.* Palgrave Macmillan.

15 Clanchy, K. (2022) *Some Kids I Taught and What They Taught Me.* Swift Press.

16 Taylor, A. (2021) 'Kate Clanchy: author to rewrite memoir amid race and ableism row', *BBC News*, 10 August, https://www.bbc.co.uk/news/entertainment-arts-58151144.

17 Rudra, P. (2022) 'What Kate Clanchy's treatment can teach us about racism', *New Statesman*, 20 June.

18 Nagesh, A. (2024) 'How woman with coconut placard was tracked down, taken to court – and acquitted', *BBC News*, 14 September, https://www.bbc.co.uk/news/articles/cvgwew5v4qyo.

19 Obese-Jecty, B. (2022) 'I'm a Black conservative. The racist abuse I receive from Black people is shocking', *Newsweek*, 26 July.

20 Abbey, N. (2024) 'Why was a Black man put on trial for using a raccoon emoji?' *The Lead*, 14 March, https://thelead.uk/why-was-black-man-put-trial-using-raccoon-emoji.

21 See https://www.cps.gov.uk/crime-info/hate-crime. The five categories of prejudice mentioned in this definition (based on disability,

race, religion, sexual orientation and transgender identity) relate to five of the nine characteristics which are protected under the Equality Act 2010 (though in the Act the protected characteristic is not 'transgender identity' but 'gender reassignment'). The other protected characteristics are age, sex, marital/civil partnership status and pregnancy/maternity.

22 A number of cases have been reported by the media in which complaints about name-calling by schoolchildren resulted in the police recording or considering recording a NCHI; in one such case a group of schoolchildren had said a classmate 'smelled like fish', while in another a child had been called 'a leprechaun'.

23 See Coates, J. (2024) '"Recording non-crime hate incidents can be a distraction for officers" – senior policing figure', *The Standard*, 16 December.

24 The judgment can be read at https://www.judiciary.uk/wp-content/uploads/2022/07/Miller-v-College-of-Policing-judgment-201221.pdf

25 As I write there is no national data on the period since new guidance was introduced, but figures released by the Metropolitan Police in London for the period June 2022 to April 2024 show a similar monthly rate of recorded NCHIs after the change as before it. These figures can be downloaded at https://www.met.police.uk/foi-ai/metropolitan-police/disclosure-2024/july-2024/non-crime-hate-incidents-june2022-april2024.

26 His Majesty's Inspectorate of Constabulary, Fire and Rescue Services (2024) *An Inspection into Activism and Impartiality in Policing*, 10 September, https://hmicfrs.justiceinspectorates.gov.uk/publication-html/activism-and-impartiality-in-policing.

27 Details are available at https://engage.vic.gov.au/anti-vilification-reforms.

28 Such double standards are visible on both the left and the right. 'Woke' leftists have defended speech which is threatening and could incite violence (e.g., 'if you see a TERF, punch them in the fucking face', uttered by a speaker to a crowd at a Trans Pride event in 2023) as just legitimate expressions of an oppressed

group's anger, while also arguing that less overtly threatening forms of offensive speech directed towards the group in question, such as misgendering, are hate speech and should incur legal sanctions. See Kirk, T. (2023) 'Trans activist Sarah Jane Baker found not guilty of encouraging violence in "punch a terf" speech', *Evening Standard*, 31 August. Conversely, right-wing activists have maintained that participants in the 2024 English riots were merely voicing 'legitimate concerns' when they made statements threatening migrants and Muslims, and should not have been prosecuted, yet characterized a black politician's statement that she would only give interviews to journalists of colour as hate speech. See Ma, C. and Conroy, M. (2022) '"Your kids are being taught an anti-white curriculum": victimhood, moral panic and the mainstreaming of racial resentment on YouTube', Oxford Internet Institute, 8 September, https://www.oii.ox.ac.uk/news-events/your-kids-are-being-taught-an-anti-white-curriculum.

29 See Higson-Bliss, L. (2024) 'Scotland's hate crime law: the problem with using public order laws to govern online speech', *The Conversation*, 23 April, https://theconversation.com/scotlands-hate-crime-law-the-problem-with-using-public-order-laws-to-govern-online-speech-227951.

5 'Literal Violence'? Dogwhistle Politics and the Language of Harm

1 Incitement is an 'inchoate' offence, meaning that steps have been taken towards the commission of a crime but the crime has not been completed (similarly, people can be prosecuted for offences like attempted murder and conspiracy to murder where no actual murder has occurred).

2 Quoted in Wilson, R. A. (2015) 'Inciting genocide with words', *Michigan Journal of International Law* 36.2, https://repository.law.umich.edu/mjil/vol36/iss2/2.

3 Benesch, S. (2012) 'The ghost of causation in international speech crime cases'. In Dojčinović, P. (ed.) *Propaganda, War Crimes Trials and International Law*. Routledge, p. 254.

4 See Straus, S. (2004) 'How many perpetrators were there in the Rwandan genocide? An estimate', *Journal of Genocide Research* 6, pp. 85–98. A later study which compared participation rates in villages with and without radio reception concluded that broadcast propaganda did have a significant influence, but acknowledged that in many cases this was not produced by direct exposure to broadcast messages, but was a 'spillover effect' arising from local social interaction (i.e., people in villages which did not have radio reception were recruited to participate via their connections with people in neighbouring villages which did have reception). See Yanagizawa-Drott, D. (2014) 'Propaganda and conflict: evidence from the Rwandan genocide', *The Quarterly Journal of Economics* 129.4, pp. 1947–94.

5 Greenberg, J. and Pyzsczynski, T. (1985) 'The effect of an overheard ethnic slur on evaluations of the target: how to spread a social disease', *Journal of Experimental Social Psychology* 21.1, pp. 61–72.

6 The linguistic and philosophical literature on slurs is extensive, but since a lot of it pursues theoretical debates which are not directly relevant to the questions explored in this section, the discussion that follows will refer to it only briefly and selectively. For readers who want to know more, a collection that covers many of the main issues and perspectives is Sosa, D. (ed.) (2018) *Bad Words: Philosophical Perspectives on Slurs*. Oxford University Press.

7 Young, J. (2020) 'USC professor under fire after using Chinese expression students allege sounds like English slur', *CNN*, 10 September, https://edition.cnn.com/2020/09/10/us/usc-chinese-professor-racism-intl-hnk-scli/index.html.

8 Kennedy, R. (2002) *Nigger: The Strange Career of a Troublesome Word*. Pantheon Books.

9 Ibid., p. 64.

10 Ibid., pp. 94–7.

11 Cepollaro, B., Sulpizio, S. and Bianchi, C. (2019) 'How bad is it to report a slur? An empirical investigation', *Journal of Pragmatics* 146.1, pp. 32–42.

12 This argument is made, for example, by David Beaver and Jason Stanley (a linguist and a philosopher respectively), who believe that even in academic discussions of slurs writers should normally avoid mentioning the words under discussion, and by the philosopher Mark Richard. See Beaver, D. and Stanley, J. (2023) *The Politics of Language*. Princeton University Press; Richard, M. (2018) 'How do slurs mean?', in *Bad Words*, ed. Sosa. Oxford University Press, pp. 155–67.

13 Fasoli, F., Maass, A. and Carnaghi, A. (2015) 'Labeling and discrimination: do homophobic epithets foster intergroup bias?' *British Journal of Social Psychology* 54, pp. 383–93.

14 Fasoli, F., Paladino, M. P., Carnaghi, A., Jetten, J., Bastian, B., and Bain, P. G. (2016) 'Not "just words": exposure to homophobic epithets leads to dehumanizing and physical distancing from gay men', *European Journal of Social Psychology* 46, pp. 237–48.

15 Struiksma, M., De Mulder, N. M. and Van Berkum, J. J. A. (2022) 'Do people get used to insulting language?' *Frontiers in Communication*, 18 July, https://www.frontiersin.org/journals/communication/articles/10.3389/fcomm.2022.910023/full.

16 Sue, D. W. (2010) *Microaggressions in Everyday Life: Race, Gender and Sexual Orientation*. Wiley, p. 5. This definition has had considerable influence on DEI policies and training in businesses and universities, but it has been criticized by some academic researchers for lacking clarity. Another recurring criticism is that both the scholarly literature on microaggressions and training materials based on that literature rely on assumptions or assertions about their harmful effects which are not supported by robust evidence. See, e.g., Lilienfeld, S. O. (2017) 'Microaggressions: strong claims, inadequate evidence', *Perspectives on Psychological Science* 12.1, pp. 138–69.

17 The examples in this section are taken from Campbell and Manning, *The Rise of Victimhood Culture*.

18 For a discussion of the legal issues (including compelled speech) raised by pronoun-sharing policies in the UK see Legal Feminist Collective (2020) 'Pronouns: compulsion and controversy', *Legal*

Feminist Blog, 19 July, https://www.legalfeminist.org.uk/2020 /07/19/pronouns-compulsion-and-controversy. In this area there have also been cases of 'compelled silence'. In 2025, the Trump administration prohibited pronoun-sharing by federal employees, but this was not the first time that had happened in the US: in 2023, Houghton University, a Methodist institution, fired two staff members for refusing to comply with an instruction to remove pronouns from their email signatures. See Sellers, M. (2023) 'Pronouns in emails get employees sacked', *HRD Magazine*, 22 May, https://www.hcamag.com/us/speciali zation/diversity-inclusion/pronouns-in-emails-get-employees -sacked/446681.

19 In *The Rise of Victimhood Culture*, Campbell and Manning cite several cases where a campus statue of a problematic historical figure has been said to make some students feel unsafe. The statue referred to here, which is mounted on the façade of Oriel College, Oxford (where Rhodes was a student, and to which he left a large sum of money), has been the object of a long-running but so far unsuccessful campaign to get it removed.

20 Barrett, L. F. (2017) 'When is speech violence?' *New York Times*, July 14.

21 Teicher, M. H., Samson, J. A., Sheu, Y. S., Polcari, A. and, McGreenery, C. E. (2010) 'Hurtful words: association of exposure to peer verbal abuse with elevated psychiatric symptom scores and corpus callosum abnormalities', *American Journal of Psychiatry* 167.12, pp. 1464–71.

22 Cohen, D., Nisbett, R. E., Bowdle, B. and Schwartz, N. (1996) 'Insult, aggression, and the Southern culture of honor: an experimental ethnography', *Journal of Personality and Social Psychology* 70.5, pp. 945–96.

23 Campbell and Manning, *The Rise of Victimhood Culture.*

24 Haslam, 'Concept creep', p. 1.

25 Dobbin, F. and Kalev, A. (2018) 'Why doesn't diversity training work? The challenge for industry and academia', *Anthropology Now* 10, p. 49.

26 Researchers who criticize anti-bias training do not suggest that there is nothing organizations can usefully do to reduce bias, inequality and conflict. Their argument is rather that institutional policies should be informed by evidence: whereas attempts to eliminate bias from individuals' minds have repeatedly been found to work poorly, initiatives which focus on changing structures, systems and procedures have been shown to produce better outcomes.

6 #LanguageMatters

1 Al-Gharbi, *We Have Never Been Woke*, p. 297.

2 Major US companies that have scaled back or eliminated DEI programmes include Alphabet (the parent company of Google), Amazon, McDonald's, Meta, Target and Walmart. See Murray, C. (2025) 'IBM reportedly walks back diversity policies, citing "inherent tensions": here are all the companies rolling back DEI Programs', *Forbes*, 11 April, https://www.forbes.com/sites/conor murray/2025/04/11/ibm-reportedly-walks-back-diversity-polici es-citing-inherent-tensions-here-are-all-the-companies-rolling -back-dei-programs.

3 Bauder, D. (2025) 'AP reporter and photographer barred from Air Force One over "Gulf of Mexico" terminology dispute', *AP News*, 15 February, https://apnews.com/article/trump-ap-news -ban-air-force-one-b90b8b842d63aef9960ccffb4a657dc2.

4 Connolly, A. J. (2025) 'Federal government's growing banned words list is chilling act of censorship', *PEN America*, 28 April, https://pen.org/banned-words-list.

5 The archived files said to have been removed included a 2015 video presentation on plain writing which advised that using the pronoun *you*, rather than phrases like 'the purchaser' or 'the beneficiary', would make the content easier for readers to understand; this seems to have been an over-zealous application of the administration's ban on using (third-person) pronouns as signifiers of gender identity. See Koebler, J. (2025) 'Trump admin deletes video explaining grammatical concept of pronouns in

war against DEI', *404 Media*, 30 January, https://www.404media
.co/trump-admin-deletes-video-explaining-grammatical-conce
pt-of-pronouns-in-war-against-dei/?utm_source=substack&u
tm_medium=email. In the same category of absurdity was the
removal from a Defense Department database of a file containing photographs of Enola Gay, the B-29 bomber that was
used to drop the world's first nuclear weapon on Hiroshima in
1945.

6 The gesture was ambiguous, resembling a Nazi salute in some
respects but clearly differing from the canonical version. Whether
it was an intentional provocation is something I find hard to
judge: Musk certainly has a record of provocative speech and
behaviour, but he also appears (like Trump) to have poor impulse
control, making it unclear how much deliberate calculation is
involved. The Anti-Defamation League (an organization that
knows a thing or two about Nazism) concluded that the salute
was probably 'an awkward gesture' rather than an intentionally
fascist one. But as with Greta Thunberg's octopus (discussed in
Chapter 3), viewers tended to interpret it to suit their preferred
political narrative.

7 Ravishankar, R. A. (2020) 'Why you need to stop using these
words and phrases', *Harvard Business Review*, 20 December,
https://hbr.org/2020/12/why-you-need-to-stop-using-these-wo
rds-and-phrases.

8 This is based on the folk-etymological claim that the word *picnic*
derives from 'pick a N----'. In fact it is an anglicized form of French
pique-nique. However, the website of the Jim Crow Museum
at Ferris State University in Michigan reproduces numerous
examples of the phrase 'lynching picnic' in texts from the era
when lynchings were a regular occurrence in the US South, and
were treated by many white people as a form of entertainment:
it meant a picnic (i.e., an outdoor gathering with food and drink)
held in the vicinity of a lynching. See https://jimcrowmuseum.fer
ris.edu/question/2021/july.htm.

9 This is a folk-legend that appears to have started among some

feminists in the 1970s and become a 'zombie fact' (one that no amount of debunking can kill). In fact the expression 'rule of thumb' most likely alludes to the historical practice among craftspeople of measuring without an actual rule[r] by treating the thickness of a thumb as approximately equivalent to one inch.

10 See McWhorter, J. (2021) 'Even *trigger warning* is now off-limits', *The Atlantic*, 4 July.

11 For a discussion of this evidence see Cameron, D. (2024) *Language, Sexism and Misogyny*. Routledge, ch. 4.

12 Gaucher, D., Friesen, J. and Kay, A. C. (2011) 'Evidence that gendered wording in job advertisements exists and sustains gender inequality', *Journal of Personality and Social Psychology* 101.1, pp. 109–28; see also Bohnet, I. (2015) *What Works: Gender Equality By Design*. Harvard University Press.

13 Polls have typically found that *Latinx* is unpopular among Spanish speakers and people of Hispanic descent in the US. See Contreras, R. (2022) 'Latino groups want to do away with "Latinx"', *Axios*, 4 January, https://www.axios.com/2022/01/04/the-rise-and-fall-latinx-latino-hispanic?utm_source=newsletter&utm_medium=email&utm_campaign=newsletter_axiosam&stream=top. Some surveys have shown resistance to *queer* among gay men and lesbians, especially those old enough to remember when it was a standard term of homophobic abuse – and who are perhaps understandably irritated by criticism from members of a generation that did not grow up with the same level of prejudice, abuse and violence. See, e.g., LGB Alliance (2023) 'Don't call me queer', https://lgballiance.org.uk/wp-content/uploads/2023/10/LGB_Queer-Report.pdf.

14 The OED's earliest citation for *parenting* is dated 1918, but it was rarely used before the 1960s. Since then it has become steadily more common: in the OED's corpus of contemporary written English, its frequency stands at three tokens per million words, compared to 0.3 tokens per million words for *mothering*.

15 *Fathering* would have been less apt for this purpose, because it is

generally used to refer to the male act of procreation rather than the activity of caring for a child.

16 Concern about 'woke' language excluding people who either struggle with reading or know very little English is in my view a red herring, since for those groups the problem isn't just obscure terminology: replacing jargon with plainer words still won't make a written text accessible to someone who isn't literate, or an English text decodable by someone who doesn't speak English. Those people need to be able to access materials in other media and/or in their own first languages. (This is of course not news either to community activists or to organizations like the UK's NHS which serve a multiethnic and multilingual population.)

17 See, e.g., Perry, L. (2021) 'Why using gender-neutral language risks excluding one minority to include another', *New Statesman*, 17 February.

18 See, e.g., Gribble, K. D. et al. (2022) 'Effective communication about pregnancy, birth, lactation, breastfeeding and newborn care: the importance of sexed language', *Global Frontiers in Women's Health*, 7 February, https://www.frontiersin.org/jour nals/global-womens-health/articles/10.3389/fgwh.2022.818856 /full.

19 Biggs, M. (2024) 'Gender identity in the 2021 Census of England and Wales: how a flawed question created spurious data', *Sociology* 58.6, pp. 1305–1323.

20 Office for Statistics Regulation (2024) *Review of Statistics on Gender Identity Based on Data Collected as Part of the 2021 England and Wales Census: Final Report*, 12 September, https:// osr.statisticsauthority.gov.uk/publication/review-of-statistics -on-gender-identity-based-on-data-collected-as-part-of-the-20 21-england-and-wales-census-final-report.

21 Kabbara, K. (2022) '14 times celebrities got called out and actu- ally made the apology, or change, people wanted', *Buzzfeed*, 26 August, https://www.buzzfeed.com/kasimkabbara/14-times- celebs-got-called-out-and-actually-made-the.

22 Cameron, *Verbal Hygiene*.

23 This policy was announced on 6 May 2025: it will apply to all the county councils which Reform won control of in elections held at the beginning of that month.